Guerrilla Publishing

How To Become A Published Author For Less Than $1500 & Keep 100% Of Your Profits

By Barbara With

Mad Island Communications
La Pointe, WI

Guerrilla Publishing
How To Become A Published Author For Less Than $1500 & Keep 100% Of Your Profits

© 2011 Barbara With

ISBN 978-0-9661378-7-3
Library of Congress Control Number: 2010912705

All rights reserved. No part of this book may be used or reproduced in any manner whatsoever without written permission.

For information, address
Mad Island Communications
P.O. Box 153
La Pointe, WI 54850
715.209.5471

www.barbarawith.com

Cover design: Holly Adams
Inside design: Barbara With
Inside Back Photo: Lois Carlson

Acknowledgments

A generous thanks goes to the La Pointe Center for funding this project; to Debbie Reinertson and Cathy Kline for being concise and conscientious editors; to Holly Adams, the best darn book designer I have ever worked with; and to Ludlow North, Jr., my devoted mentor in writing and life, as well as death.

This book is dedicated to my mother, who encouraged me to be as independent and free thinking as possible, who supported my comings and going through rock and roll and never failed to believe in me, no matter what.

Table of Contents

INTRODUCTION: If I had a dollar..................I

Part One: Writing

Chapter One: Intention & Action 9

Chapter Two: Game Plan 25

Chapter Three: Needs & Resources..................... 33

Part Two: Publishing

Chapter Four: Publish vs. Published 51

Chapter Five: The Project Matrix........................ 69

Chapter Six: Vital Statistics 83

Part Three: Selling

Chapter Seven: Oprah 97

Chapter Eight: Blue Ocean.................................. 103

EPILOGUE: If You Build It, They Can Come........115

If I had a Dollar...

Have you ever dreamt of becoming a published author? Inevitably, when people find out I'm one, nine out of ten tell me they have. Seems like everyone has a story to tell, like the salesman at the furniture store in Corpus Christi. He took 45 minutes to write the invoice for my desk while he told me the story of his grandfather he swore he would turn into a book someday. I was impressed, I admit, as he dramatically spun his yarn right there in the store.

When he was done, obviously proud of his impromptu theater, I told him what I tell every author wannabe: *write it down*. Don't recite it to everyone you meet and talk about how *someday* you're going to write this book. Sit down at the computer and write it down. Once you get it down, edit it several hundred times, hire someone else to edit, lay it out into a book and then print it. Voila: you're a published author.

Most of the world doesn't understand how easy it is to become a published author and keep 100% of the profits from every book you sell. However, the only route to becoming a published author is to write the book.

Surprisingly it doesn't necessarily begin with a great story. It starts with the discipline and commitment to finish writing any story, and then creating a structure that supports the sale of that story in the form of a book.

I offer here what I've learned from my life in publishing—Mad Island Music, founded in 1984, publishes my original songs, and Mad Island Communications was added in 1998 to publish books.

I was lucky enough to witness the end of a grand era in book publishing, as the old world art of the printed page was forced to join the digital age. When this shift happened about the time my first book came out, control was just beginning to flow back to the authors, what with the selling, networking, marketing and global power of the Internet. Add print-on-demand coming of age, and publishing is now an entirely new ball game than it was even ten years ago.

This book is not a "how-to" for starting a traditional publishing company to compete in the market of selling books. I can point you in the right direction for that: I used Dan Poynter's *Self-Publishing Manual*. His is a complete compilation of facts, processes, and rules for selling books in the traditional publishing world: timelines for release, how to get reviewed, distribution, wholesaling, book clubs, promotion and networking, etc. His is not the only one. Why reinvent the wheel?

This book is about what I call *guerrilla publishing*, as it were, built on your time, energy and imagination rather than a large budget and traditional process. I'll show you how your book can become much more than just a book for sale; it can be a calling card, an introduction, an additional revenue stream, a sample of other offerings, a platform to speak about, a fundraiser for your favorite charity, a family history, and any other myriad of uses we can think up to help you build the life you dream to live of becoming a published author.

My book is about focus and inspiration: how to finish writing, get your manuscript into book form, and allow that book to lead you. Once you have your completed book in hand, you can pursue the path of traditional self-publishing, if that's what you wish. You can shop your book to major publishers, if that's what you want. Your book will help you get speaking engagements and publicity. Even if you "just" print copies for your family and friends, it will still be worth all the work, effort and investment to become a published author.

Technology has made it possible to publish a book, own all the rights, have distribution channels in place to sell it around the world, and deliver the money to your bank account while you sleep, all the while creating a name for yourself as a published author.

> In this book you will learn:
> - ✓ Why you are publishing a book;
> - ✓ How to identify the story you want to tell;
> - ✓ How to inspire yourself to finish writing your manuscript;
> - ✓ How to design the book and create an electronic file for the printer;
> - ✓ How to set up delivery and payment;
> - ✓ How to get international distribution;
> - ✓ How to use your book in creative ways to promote a bigger life for yourself.

Part One is a how-to guide to inspire yourself to find the time, commitment and imagination to write and finish your manuscript. You'll think outside the box to find the inspiration to write every day and creative ways to organize your material into the final product, a finished manuscript.

Part Two is about how to take your manuscript and publish it into book form, then set up systems to make it available to the public.

Part Three is about how to use your book to promote yourself and your message on a larger scale, and keep 100% of all the profits from every book you sell.

IV Guerrilla Publishing

I'll dispel some common myths about today's publishing; explain the "food chain" and how traditional publishing sells books; show you creative ways around the middlemen; and inspire you to broaden your platform with other products and services.

No longer do you have to wait for a publisher to decide your book is good enough to print. Never again will a publisher change the design of the cover without your permission. Never will you be faced with your publisher deciding to discontinue printing your book and "pulping" the remainders of your inventory (another word for recycling). I will reveal to you the secrets of today's publishing world, and how easy, respectable and profitable it can be to be a self-published author.

But nothing will happen until you *write it down.*

Have you dreamt of being a published author? Then why not make it happen? You only live once. So what's it going to take to get you to carve out time in your day to sit down and work? That is the biggest challenge any future published author faces.

Once you take that step, so many more things are possible. As I remind myself, I can't win the lottery if I don't buy a ticket. You can't be an author if you don't have a published book. You can't sell books if you don't have one to sell.

When you are done reading, hopefully you will have the knowledge, inspiration and motivation to make your dream come true of becoming a published author. Regardless if your book gets onto the New York Times Best Seller list, you will have accomplished what nine out of ten people only dream of.

And trust me, the first time you hold a copy of your book in your hands, you can reap the rewards of your hard work by celebrating the fact that you are a published author! And you did it all yourself! And…you have complete control and get to keep 100% of the profits! Woo hoo!

Barbara With
Madeline Island, Wisconsin, 2010

PART ONE: Writing

CHAPTER ONE: Intention and Action

Deep within every human lives the urge to create. Whether it's art, music, writing, having children, decorating, designing, cooking, sewing or any other of a myriad of activities that build something out of nothing, we as humans are birthed with a creative instinct. Perhaps because our own bodies began as nothing but a spark between a sperm and an egg are we predisposed to creating.

Whatever the reason, I firmly believe that you have everything you need within you to create any of your dreams to come true, as long as it's objectively possible. I could not, for example, ever become the first man on the moon. But if it's doable, with enough fortitude, stamina, commitment and discipline (all character traits that can be nurtured) you can do anything you set your mind to (including nurturing these character traits). Part of this process is learning to get out of your own way and let this creative force guide you.

This powerful force of creation living within you can be frightening. In the middle of your work-a-day, orderly, routine world comes an energy that cannot and should not be tamed.

Creative force is best spontaneous, unfettered and stubborn, and yet, how do you control it to abide by your very practical schedule of job, children and real world obligations?

Before anything can happen, you need to find your muse. Without your muse, the compartmentalization of daily life will stop you before you've even begun. When the going gets tough, it's your muse who keeps you going.

What is a Muse?

According to the Greeks, there are nine goddesses who inspire the creation of literature and the arts called Muses. Their lyric poems and mythology were considered the source of all knowledge. In modern times, a muse is a part of you that keeps you absorbed in your thoughts and engaged in the machinations of writing your book. In short, it is a personification of your passion.

Since I was a child, I've had this unearthly drive to create. If I didn't write, something inside would get so bottled up I'd swear I'd go insane. Words and music then poured out of me; I cared less if it was "good" or not. All I knew was, if I didn't write, I'd get antsy and distracted and unhappy until I did.

This undeniable need to write was more to release pent-up emotion than to create a salable product. Because of this, my work acquired an originality all its own. Finding my voice was about survival, and out of survival has risen what I consider a strong, poetic and passionate voice that stands apart from the crowd.

So perhaps survival was my first muse. Later, other people and often Eros, goddess of love, was frequently my muse. Today, I am much inspired by the muse of accomplishment, addiction to achievement, and the character-building challenges of self-fulfillment. What makes me happy? To live life as a creator of art, beauty and wisdom.

On your journey to becoming an author you must find your own inspiration—someone you admire who you want to emulate; a cause; a state of being (that antsy joy of not being able to stop writing); an actual state (when I went to a hotel in Madison, Wisconsin near the capitol building to write about John Kennedy, Jr.); meditation; journaling and blogging; exercise; travel—there are infinite pathways to inspiration.

Let's identify two muses that will keep you inspired to going back to the task of writing your book.

The Muse of Love

I believe love is the most powerful muse of all. What is love? Do we need to be "in love" with someone else to find great inspiration? Often times, that flighty, giddy experience of discovering a new love can inspire great works of art. But I am referring to a kind of personal unrequited love that drives you to have to do something to satisfy its calling.

Let's take a definition of "love" from dictionary.com:

To need or require; benefit greatly from: "Plants love sunlight."

In this usage, love is a need, a longing that must be fulfilled, and in its fulfillment there is great benefit. Plants do love sun, but they also need it. Without it, they wither and die. So is true of creativity.

To allow yourself to long for something (becoming a published author) can be uncomfortable and bring out the critic in you. But the longing is what keeps you connected to your passion.

The trouble is when you allow yourself to long for something, you stir up critical thinking about how that longing can't be fulfilled. Fear of failure, or more likely, fear of success creates discouraging stories of your lack of talent that causes you to stop writing. Other thoughts will tell you it's wrong to long for something. The trick becomes to allow the emotion of longing to move through you, but change the thoughts concerning the longing.

Longing is your passion. It's more than just an idea about what you want to accomplish. Being passionate is about allowing the somewhat uncomfortable emotion of longing to flow through you to motivate you to do something about it. When you long for something, motivation is created.

As you give yourself permission to feel your longing and passion, with it comes the voice of the muse instructing you—which direction to go, what color to mix, what adjective to use, what note to play. The voice of your muse is like instinct or intuition: you may not hear the words, "Play B flat," you will just play that note because it feels right.

Think of love as that big bundle of emotions needed to impel the creation of your work. Remember, we are making something from nothing as we write. We are, in essence, the God of the story: we say who, we say when, we say how much.

The overflowing emotion in childhood compelled me to create. At age 12, I do not remember what inspired me to take the sad poem I had written and make up a melody, then put chords of a piano under that to create my first song. It was pure muse, intuition at its finest, leading me. All I had to do was listen and implement its impelling. Out of the need to write a song about the pain of my war-torn childhood came the love of creating. It's why artists traditionally are tortured. Emotion (our passion) fuels the muse's fire, and the subsequent expression somehow makes life bearable.

Following the Muse

To allow the muse of love to move through you without so much of longing's torture, stop, take a big deep breath, get out of your head, and let yourself feel. Everything. Listen to the sounds of the world around you in that moment. Don't block any emotion: let the anger, frustration or anxiety flow. Let it move through your body by breathing. Stop thinking. Actually pay attention to your breath moving through your lungs; feel the temperature of your skin; feel the ache in your knee; feel your fear. Feel whatever emotion is present, good or bad. All are part of the creative process. Revel in this uncomfortable chaos of potential without paying too much mind to the stories in your head.

Finding Your Voice

This chaos is the perfect place to begin to find your own voice. These first baby steps are the gestation period, as you are being given an opportunity to listen to yourself in a new way.

When you feel anxious, pay attention to the critical voice in your head. If it's telling you something negative or demeaning, insinuating that you can't write, then argue. With yourself. Yes, you heard me right: Have an argument with yourself. But while you are bantering around in your head, pay attention to the stories that you are telling yourself.

If you come up against the story that you just don't have time to write, respond with, "I can make the time." If you then state that you don't know enough about grammar and sentence structure, say, "I will learn." When you convince yourself you just won't follow through with finishing, because you never finish anything, proclaim, "I can do anything I set my mind to."

In this small, simple, personal way, you are finding your voice. Go for it! Stick up for yourself, with passion. State your intention. "I'll show you!" Find a new story, "I fully intend to learn whatever I need to know to become a published author." Start to weed out the self-limiting thoughts about your lack of creative power. Let the emotions of failure/embarrassment/powerlessness become like electricity and move through your body with your breath. Then choose to think new, regenerative thoughts. Tell a new story.

To keep the energy moving through you like a river, close your eyes and breathe! Let yourself feel your feelings! They will bring the voice of your Muse, telling you the next step.

Writing under the influence of the muse of love will be a relief. As you actually encourage your emotions to flow and use them to become your expression, something inside is released. These baby steps lead to renewed belief in self and excitement about actually accomplishing your dream of becoming a published author.

Writing Exercise ....

Make a list of any negative, limiting thoughts you might be having that keep you from feeling your passion:

"Who do I think I am trying to be a writer?"
"I will never become published."
"It's all been said by other people."

Create new sound bytes to use as counterpoints in your internal argument:
"I can do anything I set my mind to."
"What I don't know, I will learn as I go."
"No one can say it like me."

Allow yourself to feel your fear, but get those critical thoughts out of the way. Ask your fear to guide you. In this way you find your stride and can throw yourself into your work.

As you revel in the relief of releasing all this pent-up energy, you discover one of the greatest secrets to becoming a writer: tapping into "nothing" (the unlimited source of emotion within) and turning it into "something" (a finished manuscript).

This is the act of creation, a demonstration of self-love, and will also bring you the joys of self-validation and self-care.

The Muse of Achievement

Think back to a time when you accomplished something huge. A seemingly small event to one person can be huge to someone else.

I took a kayaking trip once and was required to take a short water safety course. I am a fish, completely at home in and on the water. But when it came time to roll the kayak, something jammed up inside of me. Even though we were in only five feet of water 20 feet off shore, I was irrationally terrified of getting trapped upside down and drowning.

After holding up the entire class for a half hour while I sat in my kayak crying, the muse of embarrassment woke the muse of achievement and together inspired me to bite the bullet and turn 360 degrees under the kayak and back out the other side. It took five seconds and it was over. Small event, huge impact.

The muse of achievement inspires you to make a plan and then focus on the small steps that lead to the big goal. The muse of achievement will be your taskmaster. This is when writing might not be fun. So be it. You can't be a published author if you don't finish your project. Everything can't always be perfect. Sometimes writing is more of a chore than other times. Pushing through the tougher times is all part of the process of completion.

After a difficult or uninspiring session, put your work away. Chances are, while you are writing, because it feels like a chore, you might have thought it wasn't good. After some time passes, go back and read what you wrote. You might be surprised to find your work is not nearly as bad as you thought while you were writing it.

When writing becomes a chore, the muse of achievement will reward you with the strength of self-discipline, which will serve you well in all of life.

To discover what inspires you, pay attention to detail of the present moment of your life. Muses are everywhere and in everything.

Writing Exercise ....
Write about a time in your life when something inspired you to go above and beyond what you thought you could do. How can you use that muse in your plan to become a published author?

Setting Your Intention

One powerful tool of inspiration is setting an intention. How many times have you said of something you never got around to accomplishing, " I really did intend to do that!"? Some might suggest that if it didn't get done, you didn't actually intend to do it.

According to dictionary.com, intention means, "An aim that guides action." You might have *said* you would do something, but you never took action, the essence of intention. Intention is more than just thinking about doing something someday; it's about developing an aim that will lead to an action that will actually accomplish the goal.

If your goal is to become a published author, the first step is to set your intention to harness your creative force and channel it into writing. But how does this intention become a series of actions that leads to the outcome, and not just an optimistic hope or thought that never goes anywhere?

1. Make a Commitment

It's one thing to have a dream and quite another to make that dream come true. Too often we sit around wondering what will happen to us. It's why the world of online psychics is so profitable: humans feel so out of control of their lives and want someone else to tell them what "fate" has in store.

To be a published author, you don't rely on fate. You use your free will to guide your own life and make decisions, every day, that lead to an end goal. You have a plan, a passion and now you must make a commitment, right out loud, that you are going to publish a book.

2. Write About Your Dream

While you don't want to get stuck just dreaming about becoming a published author, you need to ask yourself questions and begin to visualize your life as an author. Before you even begin writing your project, set aside some time to meditate on seeing yourself as a published author. Don't worry about how this dream will come true, just give yourself permission to visualize that it has.

Do you know what you want to write about? Think about what story you want to tell and why. At this point, just outline the basics. If you don't have a story, is there something you have a personal passion for that makes you want to write about it? Is it fiction or non-fiction? If it's non-fiction is it a personal experience, talent or know-how you want to articulate? Do you know this process well or is it just an idea?

Will you speak from first or second person? Knowing what party will be speaking begins to shape the voice of the work. To speak as "I did" is a very personal viewpoint, but sometimes historical and classical literature speaks more effectively with a narrator describing what "they did." Start to get a feel for which perception feels the most authentic.

Writing Exercise ....
Write a short essay on any or all of the following questions:
- What do you want to accomplish by publishing your book?
- Do you intend to publish your book for your grandchildren, friends and family, or do you dream of making a living as an author?
- If you dream of becoming a successful author, where do you see it taking you?
- Do you want to travel on a book tour? Make speaking engagements?
- What is ultimately leading you to publish?

---

3. Make Space for Your Muse

In order to develop an addiction to writing, creating an attractive, stimulating and inspiring space in which to work is essential to lure your muse out of hiding. Honestly, I do 91% of my writing in bed. In this way, I can be inspired to basically write anywhere I happen to be in the world. I made my "happy muse" space portable.

Where do you see yourself doing your writing? Imagine an inspiring workspace so perfect that you long to be there now: where is it? Are you looking out on mountains, a city scape, or some other inspiring scene? For me, the idea of getting to stay in bed all day is very appealing, and I can do it everywhere.

Now, imagine you are there, finally with nothing to do but focus on your writing. You don't have to do anything but allow your muse to emerge and inspire you to write. Start longing for this.

In the popular television series, *Sex and The City*, Carrie Bradshaw's space wasn't inspired by her view of West 78th Street as much as her love affair with New York City. Her muse lived on the streets of Manhattan. She organized her home to accommodate her need to write: she lived alone, her house was simple and comfortable, her desk an uncluttered space set aside just for writing. Since she was childless, single and getting paid to be a writer, she lived by her own hours and was always looking around New York for inspiration for her next column.

My work has allowed me to follow my travel muse on writing adventures. To finish my second book, *Party of Twelve: The Afterlife Interviews*, for four months I traveled every other week from Minneapolis, Minnesota to Madison, Wisconsin. Each weekend my girlfriend and I would make the drive and check in the same hotel near the capitol. After a while we got a reputation with the staff. (If you want to generate mystique, tell the staff of your hotel that you are an author come to write your next book.)

While Sissy was off with her lover, I would hole up in the room and write. With room service, breaks at the rooftop bar to slurp champagne and the hot tub by the pool, a great book came out of me. The muses of love, achievement, and travel ganged up on me to inspire the perfect manifestation of living the writer's life. And the entire experience was part of the magnificent journey of becoming a published author.

> *Writing Exercise* ....
> What does your sacred workspace look like and how will it continue to inspire you?

4. How Big is Your Platform?

If you dream of becoming a professional writer, do you have a vision of work that might follow the first book (a second book, a screenplay of the book, speaking engagements and presentations, workshops associated with the book)? This is called your platform. Authors with bigger platforms have a better chance of success. Books sell workshops and workshops sell books.

My platform includes songs, books, live musical performances, a workshop called ConflictREVOLUTION®, one on Manifestation, another on Creativity, screenplays, movie treatments, and musical theater pieces. I dream that one day Celine Dion records one of my songs, and the royalties provide the money to produce my own movie, to which I will write the novel, as well as the sound track, and keep 100% of the profits.

Life is short; dream big.

5. Personal Projects

Perhaps you are someone with an ingenious idea that simply wants to create a book, just to do it. Maybe you have no interest in going any farther than just friends and family. You will still need to finish writing the book before you can do anything.

6. Your First Book

Imagine how it feels to be holding your finished book in your hands. See it, feel the texture, smell it, imagine the feeling as you crack the cover of your very first book in print. Long for the book like you would a lover.

I speak from experience when I say, no matter how many times you read your manuscript, holding your book in your hands will be like reading it for the first time. Imagine that.

> *Writing Exercise* ....
> Sketch out an informal business plan for the next five years. Have fun brainstorming possible growth and direction. Don't belabor the point; this isn't work, this is play. Imagine the biggest, most spectacular platform you can. You do want to be an author, after all. Dream about what you are doing and what your life looks like after you succeed.

Letting Go of Expectations

Now that you have taken the care to create your vision, let yourself get excited about it. Don't hold back. Enjoy what Walt Disney called the "Imagineering" process. Pour your longing into the vision of becoming a published author.

Then, when you are through with these daydreams, let them all go. However feels appropriate for you. Put them in a big balloon and pop it. Or send them in a rocket launcher to explode over the landscape and twinkle to earth like snow.

I sometimes imagine my vision contained in a firework on the end of an arrow. I imagine slowly pulling back my powerful bow and aiming the arrow into the moon. With a count down, "Three, two, one, LET GO!" I release the arrow and watch it soar against the grainy moonlight and suddenly explode into a pyrotechnic display of inspiring magnitude. Every little spark is a piece of my dream that I am releasing to the universe.

However you choose, release the vision to the universe and proceed forward with your day and whatever is on your plate. Turn your full attention to what's at hand and *let go of the expectation of the outcome of those dreams.*

Yes, you heard me. Let go of the expectation of fulfilling this dream. Instead, I will teach you to focus on *creating an expectation inside yourself that you will take an action that will lead one step closer to the desired outcome.*

Let Go

This aspect of setting an intention might be one of the most difficult to do: *letting go of the outcome while instilling the expectation that you will take an action toward the outcome.*

When you attach to the outcome, you focus on where you are now compared to this outcome you're striving for. The trouble is, where you are now seems terribly far away from where you want to be. This comparative analysis results in feelings of frustration. Clearly you see how far you have to go. One baby step does not seem to make a dent to close the gap between your dream and its manifestation.

This perspective makes the journey daunting from the start and sets up the self-talk that will lead you away from taking action towards your intention. "What's the use?" you tell yourself, "It's too far to go." This is when, without even knowing, you slip up, forget to write, get too busy, or distract yourself with other activity. This is the stuff self-sabotage is made of.

However, *instilling an expectation that you will take an action towards the outcome* refocuses your awareness off the outcome and onto something doable: one baby step towards making that dream come true, one step at a time, *right now.*

CHAPTER TWO: Game Plan

To successfully instill the expectation to go one step at a time, you must first create a plan, and then consciously make a commitment to implement the plan, one step at a time. Written into this plan are easy and achievable daily goals, ones you define for yourself. Instead of measuring your progress on how far you have to go, you celebrate how far you've come and build on that.

Slowly but surely, one step at a time, you train yourself to become addicted to success and achievement. One baby step at a time becomes the millions of little steps it takes to manifest your dream. As you focus on these steps, one day you look up and voila, you're there.

Perhaps your plan includes writing for thirty minutes three mornings a week, or setting aside time on Wednesday to work on a story idea. These small outcomes are the actual baby steps that get you to the final product. The grains of sand that become the beach; the drops of water that become the ocean.

The good news is that *you* write the plan. You make sure your plan is well thought-out and the tasks are doable, which will promote success. These small successes build on each other and inspire you to continue taking baby steps that eventually fulfill your grand intention. By making the steps doable, the muse of achievement becomes your best friend.

After seeing this remarkable vision of your life as a published author and holding your first book in your hands, you set your intention to manifest this vision into physical reality. Now let's begin creating a plan to accommodate your writing needs.

The Big Picture

Start by examining the practical details of your life and find a way, working with what you have, to make room for the needs of your muse.

Figure out within the scope of your personal life—your schedule, your living space, your obligations—where you will fit in time to write your book, and how you will take action. Don't think of it as a sacrifice; think of it as taking steps to cultivate creativity and passion, to make your life fuller, deeper, richer and more personally fulfilling.

Setting aside time to write will reconnect you with yourself. Give yourself permission to feel the self-gratification of self-discipline. It's a powerful feeling to follow-through on your plans, just because you decide you will.

Can you cut back on socializing three or four hours a week? Can you rise early, before work, and get a couple hours of writing in? Is there a place you can go during lunch—a local coffee shop or library—where you can focus only on your writing?

TURN OFF THE TELEVISION!
The average American watches four hours of television a day. That's two months a year, 24 hours a day. Turn it off. In fact, I don't even have cable. Watching TV is the worst offender of burning up precious creative hours of any invention on the planet.

Set your intentions. Write them down. Be specific. "I fully intend to spend three hours a week before work writing at the Starbuck's on Second Street." Then come up with an action plan of how you will do this (going to bed early the night before; informing your husband of your plan; setting the alarm and creating any inspirational sound bytes to use when that alarm goes off to keep you from going back to sleep).

When I was writing my third book, *Imagining Einstein: Essays on M-Theory, World Peace & The Science of Compassion*, I was living in a small cabin with my then-husband and working as a realtor fifty hours a week. We used the one bedroom for his office and slept in the living room. My "office" was a walk-in closet that was not big enough for my desk. I set my intention to find the time and space to write this book, but under these circumstances, I was indeed challenged.

I set up my computer on the dining room table and got up every day at 4 a.m. to work for four hours before heading off to work. Yes, it meant disrupting his sleep with the tick tick tick of my typing, being tired at work, and going to bed earlier, but I can tell you, it was well worth it to author that book.

Just Do It

Being an author means more than just practicing the act of writing. Many of us write in our journals, on blogs, on our Facebook pages, or for work. This does indeed make us all *writers*. But to become an *author*, you must actually *finish the book*. You move from being a writer to becoming an editor and project manager to lead the book project to completion. What you learn from this experience will affect all areas of your life. The discipline you exercise here will translate into your other projects and intentions.

You will experience the secret of highly successful people: becoming addicted to accomplishment. The personal satisfaction of finishing your manuscript will feed your muse that is hungry for expression and actualization. It's like no other high I know.

So begin to cultivate discipline. Don't just roll your eyes and tell me you just aren't that focused. Don't tell me you hate that word "discipline" because it reminds you of the nuns and their rulers. I don't want to hear it. Define discipline not as punishment, but self-love. Discipline will become your best friend and most loyal companion. State your intention to cultivate the will power and awareness to make personal choices that take you one step closer to your desired outcome. Learn to love the fulfillment that comes from staying focused on follow-though.

The good news is, you can do it any way that works for you. I set up what I call "fake deadlines" for myself, which motivate me to get going. But whatever gets you to pay attention and just do it is what you should be doing. This is your muse, after all.

Support Groups

Some writers find inspiration working with other writers in groups. Look for meetup.com groups in your neighborhood; check the local coffeehouse for groups that might meet there; the library is a great source for finding other writers interested in working together. Share your intentions with others who are as serious about writing as you are. Form a support group of your own to coach each other towards becoming published authors. Just don't spend too much time talking about it; make sure you get home and write.

Join news groups or blogs devoted to writing. Subscribe to *Writer's Digest* and other professional publications. There are many excellent books on how to get started and stay inspired. *Writing Down the Bones* by Natalie Goldberg, and *An Artist's Way* by Julie Cameron are two of my favorite. Find what tools inspire you and work with them.

Know the Basics

Every good writer needs to understand the basic elements of writing. Good grammar and spelling are essential. Pick up *Strunk's Elements of Style*, an industry standard for style formats.

As much as a good writer follows classic grammar and style elements, don't be afraid to step outside the box. Who made up the rule you cannot end a sentence with a preposition? I often ignore this, perhaps because of my last name. "Who is Barbara With?" simply must be acceptable in some format.

Henry Miller, in his ground-breaking book, *Sexus*, published in 1962, used caret symbols for quote marks. As I read, I thought to myself, <<This is very irritating.>> Some "outside the box" experiments just don't work.

Do everything you can to immerse yourself in the world of writing to keep inspiring yourself to take action. Learning more about grammar, style, usage and spelling will sharpen your focus and help shape your voice. Using the mantra "I am an author" can keep you accountable for following through on your intentions.

When in Doubt, Just Write Something

Once you have saturated yourself in your goal of becoming a published author, and mapped ways to organize your time to accomplish that goal, take action today. Even if you start with small increments, say, writing first thing in the morning for fifteen minutes, do something every single day to move your intention into an action.

I believe the biggest derailer of any goal is trying to take too large a step in the beginning. If you set an intention to run a marathon, you would not go out and run 26 miles the first day. You would create an action plan to incrementally work up to 26 miles, one mile at a time. Constantly thinking about how long 26 miles is would defeat your enthusiasm. Taking one mile at a time makes you succeed every day toward that goal.

Becoming an author means taking small steps every day, letting go of the expectation of the outcome, while instilling the expectation of the action toward the outcome. It means loving living the life of an author as much as having the final product.

Lower Your Expectations

Oddly enough, creating daily goals can be fun and rewarding when we lower our expectations in the beginning. Make a list of things you will absolutely get done today. Make them so doable it's not even funny. It's much easier to accomplish the goal to write at least ten minutes three times a week than to write four hours every morning. Make it within easy reach considering your schedule and obligations.

Then as you fulfill these daily goals, cross them off the list. At the end of the day, instead of a long list with only a few things accomplished (leaving you feeling overwhelmed and behind schedule), your list is complete and you can revel in the fact that you succeeded in what you set out to do. It doesn't matter that you would have done these tasks anyway. We are training you to getting used to fulfilling goals by making the goals achievable.

This kind of satisfaction of achievement becomes addictive. You feel so good you can eventually set daily goals that are more challenging. Because you are becoming addicted to an author's life and your book is actually coming into form, you celebrate the baby steps that are adding up to the final result of you becoming a published author.

The bottom line is, only you can decide, at 4:30 in the morning, how to get yourself out of bed, make a nice pot

---

Barbara's To-Do List for Today
- ✓ ~~Brush Teeth~~
- ✓ ~~Open mail~~
- ✓ ~~Yoga~~
- ✓ ~~Work on book at least 15 minutes~~
- ✓ ~~Beach~~

---

of coffee and start writing. Do you have that fire in your belly? If not, how will you conjure it up? In the end, it's all up to you. And that's the good news.

Choosing to take small steps everyday builds on itself as you gain self-respect and become a person of action. This is just one of the many byproducts of your journey to coming a published author.

For me, there was a cutting-edge magic present at 4 a.m. with my coffee and a picture of Einstein taped to my computer. For me, this was what being an author was all about; these were the moments I lived for. I wasn't going to miss a one.

CHAPTER THREE: Needs & Resources

You might suppose the first and most obvious need in becoming a published author is writing talent. While it certainly won't hurt, let me suggest otherwise.

One of the most powerful skills in any successful endeavor is being able to articulate what is needed to accomplish the goal, and then finding the discipline and resources to meet those needs. This skill, once learned, can serve you well in all areas of your life.

So, too, with becoming a published author. You have a specific set of circumstances that you will need to rearrange to make the commitment to accomplish your goal. You have strengths and weaknesses, skills you can utilize and skills you must outsource. The process of identifying the needs will naturally lead you to the resources for fulfilling those needs, with the proper attention paid.

What worked for me may not work for you. For example, I have graphic design skills; I'm unmarried with no children and live in an isolated place with control of my schedule. This makes it much easier for me to find the resource of time but harder to find balance. You create your own needs analysis and resource assessment based on your situation.

First, we'll define a *need* as "a lack of something deemed necessary to accomplish the goal." As you identify your needs, you can begin to match your resources to them in a thoughtful and effective way.

> *Writing Exercise* ....
> Write down all your conceivable needs when it comes to accomplishing your goal to be a published author. Brainstorm, have fun, imagine, dig deep and see how many needs you can come up with:
> - ✓ A babysitter so you can have time away from the kids;
> - ✓ Someone to design the book;
> - ✓ To be more focused in general;
> - ✓ Editing help;
> - ✓ Ways to inspire yourself to get up early and write before work;
> - ✓ Time alone;
> - ✓ Less time in front of the television.

Now let's define a *resource* as "the sum of the wealth of your life." Not just money but any source of supply, support, or aid that can be readily drawn upon when needed.

When I was working on my fourth book, *Party of Twelve: Post 9/11*, I needed a promotional picture for the cover. I didn't have much money at the time to pay a photographer, but I knew my friend Lois was in need of my consulting services. I traded her a photo session for a coaching session.

Resources are everywhere. When you start to look at all that is available to you on every level, you begin to relax and get into the flow of the project. Instead of a need becoming an insurmountable obstacle, it becomes a joyful discovery process of watching to see where a resource will arise when you ask for one. Ask and you will receive, if you pay attention with an open mind.

> *Writing Exercise* ....
> Identify your resources by listing absolutely everything you can think of that is a part of your source, support or assistance:
> - ✓ Your six weeks of accrued vacation you could use to take a trip solely to focus on writing;
> - ✓ Your sister-in-law, who can take the kids one day a week;
> - ✓ Your cousin with the graphic design business;
> - ✓ The spare room over the garage to use as a writing space.

Some needs may not have a resource, yet. But by articulating the need, you have effectively asked the universe to provide. Always remember, there is infinite abundance, and so many resources yet undiscovered that could fill your need when the time comes, so don't worry. If you find yourself worrying, stop, take a breath, move that worrisome energy through you and remind yourself, the resource will be made manifest, all in good time. Work with what you have, and more than likely, that's a gracious plenty.

Time Management

Begin by looking at your life as it is. What do you spend your time doing? How much is required to run the details of your existing life? How much do you work? Shop? Take care of family? Volunteer? Socialize with friends? How much time do you spend reading and watching movies? How often is the television on in the background?

If it helps, get a calendar and fill in what you actually did last week. See where there is any time left for working as a writer. More than likely there is very little.

Don't be daunted. This means nothing except that you have not yet created the time to devote to your writing and your goal. It doesn't mean there isn't room; it just means you have to rearrange to make room. Like getting a new couch that won't fit against the wall where the old one sat. You need to pull everything out of the room and put it back in a new configuration. The same is true of making time for writing.

Once you get this overview, begin to assess your needs. What is absolutely essential (picking up the kids from school) and where you can cut back doing particular activities for a while (happy hour at Bunny's). Don't make the mistake of thinking to be an author means no social life, or having to write at odd hours. While you are writing the book, yes, you might not go to as many movies as you normally do. But just for the duration of the project, and then you can catch up with rentals. These are the kinds of "sacrifices" worth making.

As much as you love hanging out at Bunny's having beers with the girls, maybe some nights you can stay home and write. Discipline does not have to mean unpleasant sacrifice. What you sacrifice in not doing the normal activities will be rewarded with the deep personal satisfaction and fulfillment of actually doing what you say you will. You'll be feeding your muse, exercising your creative power, and taking baby steps toward your goal: a book with your name and your story, which will make you a published author. This is far bigger than beers at Bunny's. This is a dream come true.

These are the kinds of actions that turn the meaning of discipline from punishment to self-love. These actions will make you sleep like a baby at night, and your happy hour friends will be there when you are done, envious.

So now you've set an intention that every Tuesday morning after the kids go to school and before your schedule of afternoon appointments, you will spend three hours working on your book. You have it written into your schedule, and won't make appointments at that time, or forget and end up shopping because you happened to be passing by Macy's after you dropped the kids.

You can develop this kind of visionary self-awareness about writing. When you create a practical, serious, and doable plan and stick to it, you won't always be worrying about when you will have the time to write. Now it's like a job commitment.

After those three hours of writing, you can walk away fulfilled, proud and excited that you're living your dream, and anxious to write again.

Now that you've committed to setting aside time to write, let's look at some ways to approach the actual writing that will keep you inspired and engaged, even when the words aren't flowing, or the way is unclear.

The joy of writing is pulling words out of thin air, words that no one else has put together in quite this way, and making a story that's strong, fluid and captivating, no matter what you are writing about.

Developing a Story

My salesman friend at the furniture store already had his story developed, from beginning to end. He told it in vivid detail; being that it was about his grandfather, he merely had to recite the events of his life. Not everyone has this clear a story. This is where strong story development on the front end will make writing more manageable and fun.

One trick of the trade is to first write what is called a treatment. In the movie industry, a treatment is the story of what the movie will be about, an outline for the screenwriter to develop the script. Anywhere from three to 25 pages, the treatment tells only as much detail as is needed to easily cover the salient points to be expanded later in the writing process. Consider it a short story that will be used to outline the bigger structure of your writing project.

Some authors let the story tell itself as they go; others outline each twist and turn beforehand. There are even software programs that will coach you in story development.

Whether you're telling the story of your life, or a completely fictional tale, there are basic elements of all stories on which the telling is built. If you have these elements, your structure will be sound and it can rise up and write itself.

Conflict

Yes, it's true, great stories have great conflict. The Protagonist(s) (the heroes and central figures of the story) are at odds with the Antagonist(s) (the adversary opposing and contending with the hero). Out of this human struggle arises the drama you're looking for to tell a riveting tale.

Don't shy away from drama or conflict. Use it to make the story more colorful and captivating.

A Comprehensive Introduction

How you open your story has a powerful impact on what follows. Carefully consider how you set the stage. You want people to want to know more, to need to turn the page to find out what happens next. Your introduction can be as short as a paragraph, or a chapter in and of itself. The best stories hook you with the first sentence.

Set the stage with alluring appeal and you will get them hooked early.

Rising Action

Build your story well. What events and activities are the protagonists and antagonists going through? Fighting on a battlefield together? Married? Government officials trying to save the country from attack? What events are leading up to the eventual climax of your story? Set the stage and build one scene on another.

Climax

Identify what the climax of the entire story is going to be. This is perhaps the epitome of the telling, when the truth is revealed. Here the knowledge, resolution, and revelation of the conflict finally unfold fully.

Conclusion

From here, the final pieces are revealed, loose ends are tied, and your story is brought to a close. Even though the curtain goes down, sometimes the door is left open for the next volume, leaving the reader curious to know more. Either way, your last words should bring all the threads together leaving your readers satiated for having gone on your journey with you.

Whatever story you choose to write, make it one you have a personal affiliation to. Have a passion for it, and it will guide you.

Table of Contents

Once you have clearly developed your story idea or written your treatment, one of the easiest tools to organize the project is creating the table of contents. Fleshing out a TOC creates the outline you need to begin writing.

Like a business plan that guides the growth of the company, a table of contents guides the direction of the book, creating an introduction, beginning, middle, ending and epilogue, each with themes and titles to work from. However, the TOC is not meant to be carved in stone; it's merely a diagram to begin work. Expect the TOC to accommodate the changing story line.

Breaking your story out into the TOC offers the opportunity to write in a nonlinear fashion. One day you might work on the ending, the next the middle. This allows for more fluid creativity by allowing you to be drawn to what moves you to write about on any particular day. Your bits and pieces then get plugged into the plan. This flexibility increases inspiration and flow. If you are tired of talking about the protagonists, you can pick any point in the story and let your passion lead you to write about the antagonists.

The more planning done in this fashion on the front end, the more fun you will have when it comes time to write.

The Flow and The Editor

In 1987, I made a most startling discovery: I spontaneously started automatic writing. It began as a letter to my friend, telling her how "bad it was to make judgments." In one second, my thinking shifted, as if I stepped aside and let someone else do the talking. The result was writing three pages so quickly I couldn't have stopped to think about what I was saying. Yet what came out was remarkably well written for having no forethought.

Since that day, I have become a huge fan of not thinking when I write. It gets me out of my head to allow the natural flow of the story to come through. And it works for both fiction and nonfiction.

Practice flow writing any time. Just pick a topic (your high school prom, let's say) and give yourself a time limit to write on the topic: ready, set, go. Then just open your mind to the visceral memories of prom, and begin to describe what you see and sense from that recall. Don't worry if it's good or bad or if it has a plot. In fact, don't think at all, just write! See if you can get into the flow and let your fingers lead the way instead of your mind.

After you're done, go take a walk or have a cup of coffee. Come back later and read what you wrote. See what works and what doesn't. Have fun with it.

To successfully master the flow you will need to acquaint yourself well with an aspect of your personality I call the *internal editor*. This editor can be your best friend, but when cranky, can also become that critical voice saying you aren't good enough, doubting the creative process. If you don't learn how to direct this aspect of yourself, it can derail your project in a heartbeat.

The good news is the editor's job is to edit: to make sure everything is well written, succinct, captivating and fluid. You need this talent, but not while you are trying to write with the flow.

The trick to working with this editor is to get to know it well. Listen to that critical part of your brain, asking who do you think you are, pretending to be a writer? That voice that, after every sentence you write, tries to convince you to go back and re-write it because it's not good enough.

Then understand that you *need* this part of your brain *when it comes time to edit*. Don't try to banish the internal editor, instead ask it to quietly wait its turn. When the time comes, you can slice and dice to your heart's content, *but not at the point of flow.*

Your internal editor will want to read a sentence over and over before moving on to the next one. Its job is, after all, to edit the words into a tighter, more concise form. *But not during the flow.* An editor piping up during this creative output stops the flow, generally through criticism and self-doubt.

Understand there's a reason they call it a rough draft. It's supposed to be rough at this stage of the game, an information dump. Once you output enough content, perhaps several chapters, you can to go back and edit. At that time, belabor the verbiage, rearrange the ideas, delete the inane, beef up the best and shape the raw material into something stronger to your heart's content.

These doubts can be debilitating, so your job is to quiet this voice for the moment and actually encourage the chaos of brilliance, the often sloppy results of getting out of your own way and writing with the flow.

Remind yourself, there will come a time to edit. I adore the editing process. In fact, the more you edit yourself, the stronger your voice will become. Don't be afraid to take time to form and shape in this way. *But not during the flow.*

Once you understand and can separate the intention between flow and editor, you can quiet the mind when needed, and utilize your inner critic to make it better after the fact.

Authenticity

An author's voice is perhaps the most magical part of the journey of writing. Your view of life is unique. No one else can possibly see and describe the world from your perspective but you.

I have always been a big believer in being as individual as possible. I tend not go with the trends or copy the current cultural heroes. To stand aligned to your authentic self makes for a compelling voice. But therein lies the rub: who exactly is the authentic you?

When writing from a place of authenticity, you will face your most critical and unaccepting self, and this is the good news. Outing this part of your own mythology—the stories that say you aren't good enough to write this book, your voice is not strong enough, you aren't talented enough, clever enough, *fill-in-the-blank* enough—is the liberation you are seeking. Don't be afraid to admit this part of you. In facing your critical self, you can change it. You are not destined to be your own worst enemy the rest of your life; you can change.

Every experience in your life brings you potential wisdom. When you stop judging and just examine your life, like a reporter, you find episodes with rich details, deep emotion, uneasy questions that contain the gold of the experience that will shape your authentic voice.

Every single situation you've been in gives you a unique worldview. So pay attention. Quit getting so wrapped up in your own self-talk and turn your focus outward, to the world around you. Everything you need to write a great book is right here for the taking.

So speak up. Risk being bad, so you can get better.

Writer's Block

Inevitably, you will face the moment when nothing comes out of your imagination to even form words around. You will get discouraged, uninspired and dejected. Get used to it. It's all part of the flow.

Over the years, I have learned not to judge any piece of writing at the time I am writing it. Songs I swore were crap while I was composing them sounded like symphonies after I was done. While you're writing you can get so caught up on the "inside" of the work that you can't even begin to see it from the "outside." You aren't supposed to so don't even try.

Every writer gets writers block. I would be surprised if you didn't. You can save yourself a lot of sabotage if you just face it head on, and don't panic. There's a world of options that will help open the gates again.

Work on something else. I will often have two projects going at one time. When I get stuck on one, I can flip over to the other. Put your piece aside for a day or two and do something else creative that doesn't require writing. Do some yoga, take a walk, get your mind on something else and keep reminding yourself, "This too shall pass."

Monitor your internal dialogue. You might hear a lot of critiquing from the internal editor. Make sure you aren't flogging yourself needlessly, or being too harsh with yourself. Ease up and remind yourself, you will get through this, we all do. Part of what makes it a block is because our minds are telling us so.

Switch up where you write. Pack up the laptop and discover a new milieu to work. Go on your own informal writer's retreat to a spa or hotel and hole up in your room writing. A change of scenery can help start the flow again, and restore perspective.

Write it anyway. Try forcing yourself to write. If necessary resign yourself to the fact that it will be the worst crap you've ever written but celebrate that you are writing anyway. Set it aside for a few days, and then revisit it. See how much is bad writing, or how much was the critical internal editor. It's very likely you were unable to see the "outside" as clearly while you were "inside."

Write about your writer's block. Use it to explore some of the anxieties buried below the surface that are preventing you from moving forward.

Look at it like a job you just have to finish. Forge ahead knowing this, too, shall, pass. As my friend the "Accidental Guru" says: You can because you must!

Working Your Program

If you're like me, you've known for years that you wanted to be a published author. I used to write stories and create little books that I'd illustrate myself, pages bound together with big brass clips and voila, I was published at the age of twelve. But this burning urge to write carries its own set of quirks.

Writers must love, at least part of the time, being alone. Don't worry, you can still have a social life, but the act of writing requires concentration and organization of thoughts, and lots of them. If you are uncomfortable being alone with yourself, writing probably isn't for you. However, theoretically you could carry around an MP3 recorder and speak your story, then have the recording transcribed and hire an editor to shape it into form. But I'm talking about the old school pen to the paper, loitering over words, concepts and what you are passionately being called to say.

Writers like puzzles. Every word is a clue; every sentence a brainteaser; every chapter a challenge. If you're easily frustrated by puzzles, you miss the whole point of developing and articulating a story of your own. You're creating something from nothing, remember, and you're in charge. No one can solve the puzzle but you.

Writers thrive on not being one of the crowd. Developing a strong and unique voice of your own is the goal, not shaping your vision around what you think someone else believes you should do. Have the courage to stand apart, be unique, say it like it is to you and not sound like anyone else. Find your voice and speak it loud.

Writers pay attention to detail. In the movie, *Slumdog Millionaire*, the lead character went on to win the million dollars by remembering the details of what had been horrific experiences. He paid attention to details even in the worst moments, and utilized that knowledge in a clever and obviously profitable way. Writers weave real life impressions into whatever tale they are telling.

A good writer never judges what's being written while its being written. There is absolutely no way to tell if your work is good or bad in the middle of the flow. Think of it as fodder, or the clay that will eventually get carved down into form. Keep writing, and then put it aside for a few days and come back to it. It's never as bad as you think and often much better than you imagined at the time. Edit it, again and again, until it literally sings.

A published author will finish the project no matter what.
So here you are, intent on becoming a published author. You've dreamt your dreams, set your intention, rearranged your schedule, developed a story line, and charted a course to instill an expectation that you will take action every day to make your dream a reality.

Some mornings you get up early and work from home; other afternoons you slip out to the Starbucks and settle into a corner with your laptop. Each time you finish a writing session, you give yourself permission to get excited that, indeed, you're doing it. You are in the process of finishing your book.

Little by little, step by step, you write your book. When you're stumped with something, you find the resources to unstick you. You tolerate fatigue at work, a duller social life, fewer nights in front of the television in order to accomplish your dream. All the while, you are relishing living the life of a writer.

Finally, after however long it takes (it took four years to write and publish my first book; four months for my fourth) you have a finished manuscript. Your baby, this labor of love, this expression of one of your wildest dreams come true has taken place. You have actually written a book.

At this juncture, I highly recommend a night on the town, complete with champagne and lots of it. Congratulations are in order!

You have, however, only accomplished half the job you've set out to do: become a published author. Now, you must *publish*. Here's where the real fun begins!

PART TWO: Publishing

Chapter Four: Published vs. Publisher

When I was writing my first book, *Diaries of a Psychic Sorority,* in the mid 90s, old school publishing was on the cusp of a great transformation. It wasn't dead yet, but everywhere were signs that things weren't well in the world of books. At the time, my coauthors and I had to decide if we should find a literary agent to shop our book to a major publisher, or take control and publish the work ourselves.

In 1997, being self-published wasn't the worst thing that could happen. Warner Brothers had just signed James Redfield and his blockbuster *Celestine Prophesies,* but only after he self-published and drove around the country selling 100,000 copies out of the back of his car directly to bookstores and at events.

Rising overhead and declining profits were forcing publishers to eliminate public relations services offered to authors. Advances dried up, and more and more authors were being expected to pay for promotion and marketing efforts. For someone like Redfield, who proved he could sell books, the doors opened. The rest of us had to submit a detailed business plan with the exact steps that we planned to take to promote our book.

Identifying our readership as the New Age/Metaphysical market, we felt our true story held up well within the competition of Redfield, Sylvia Brown and Neale Donald Walsh. In the end, we decided to do both: we proceeded to self-publish, thereby making the work available immediately, but we also contracted with a literary agent, who began shopping our book to major publishers around the world.

Traditional Publishing Process

There is a well-defined process to getting signed by a major publisher. It begins with a submission of the finished manuscript, done either by the author or a literary agent, to a publisher who works in your genre. (If you aren't sure what genre you fall into, go into a big bookstore and find the section you would place your book. *Diaries* straddled between "self-help," and "spiritual/metaphysical.")

Submissions directly from authors are considered "unsolicited" and go into a slush pile overseen by an editorial assistant or publisher's reader who pulls out what she thinks is the best to send on to the acquisitions editor.

Literary agents have relationships with editors and pitch the concept of your book to them, along with your business plan and the first 100 pages of your manuscript. If an editor is interested, the manuscript is sent as "solicited" and the agent continues to champion it through the review process, hopefully to become accepted for publication.

The acquisitions editor sends her picks on to the editorial staff. The size of the publishing company will determine how many people along this food chain have to agree that the book has high sales potential and vote for publishing. In most cases, unsolicited materials are rarely published. Today, it might be one in every ten thousand unsolicited manuscripts that get noticed. In fact, most publishers simply will not accept unsolicited manuscripts from previously unpublished authors.

Once the manuscript is accepted, the commissioning editors are called in to negotiate the terms of the contract. An author, in essence, sells the right to reproduce her work to the publisher, and agrees on a royalty rate: the percent of gross retail sales that goes back to the author, anywhere from 2-12%.

Published vs. Publisher 53

An advance is also negotiated. Publishers must calculate potential sales and come up with an advance, which is generally 1/3 of the profits of the first print run. For example, if the print run is 5,000 and the book retails at $15.95, and the author receives 6% royalties, the total due to the author for the sale of all 5,000 books would be $4,785 ($15.95 x 5,000 = $79,750 x .06 = $4785), thus creating an advance of roughly $1,595. Advances, however, vary greatly according to size of publisher, stature of author and projected sales. Royalties are then paid after the publisher recoups the advance.

When you sign with a publisher, you basically give away the rights to the final say of what happens to your work in exchange for a very small percentage of what is sold. Out of almost $80,000 in possible revenues, you would get $4800. Although the author retains the copyright and technically owns the work, the publisher now owns the right to copy and sell it, and can do anything they wish with the material.

After deals are struck and contracts are signed, the manuscript begins its journey to be shaped by the publisher's vision. The first stop is the content editor.

Content editing involves checking the story for inconsistencies regarding characters, plot, or style, in order to create the most compelling, congruent, and consistent book possible, one that grabs the reader and pulls them in for more. At this stage, the author might be asked to rewrite plot lines, further develop characters or improve the quality of certain themes. Facts are checked and contradictions addressed. Even the title might be changed.

After content is established, the book goes into copy editing, which focuses on structure—spelling, capitalization, punctuation, tense, grammar et al. This is the last stop before the book heads to design.

Because you have licensed the rights to the work, the publisher has the final say in everything. In an ideal partnership, you and the editor work together; a good editor will make your words ring as true to your original voice as possible. But the bottom line is, publisher has final say. They can even change the title against your better judgment. Remember, you just signed away your rights.

The same is true with design. Some non-fiction works are heavily laden with illustrations and images and require more intensive attention. Works of fiction require only type and cover design decisions. Cookbooks and children's books have their own design demands. Publishers generally try to maintain a particular style standard, but design will depend on the manuscript and the editor's taste.

The publisher should prepare sales materials to promote your book through their established channels. Using cover design ideas, sell cards are created: postcards with the book cover on one side and all the vital stats about you and your book on the other. Salespeople send out cards to major and independent bookstore chains months before release with a mail-back postcard to request a free copy of your book. Information garnered from these early market tests shapes the book. Covers can be redesigned, print runs increased or decreased, and in some cases, the book itself could be dropped before it's even done.

Once the book is laid out, it's time for the print run. Traditional publishing determines the size of the print run for each title based on how much the publisher believes can be sold and the author's marketing abilities, whether it's a big name or a business plan. Printing has traditionally been done in bulk, as the more books printed, the less the cost of each book.

Let's say your publisher orders a print run of 5,000 books. The printer ships the books to the distributor, who houses the books until they are sold to wholesalers, e.g. bookstores. (Distributors do not generally sell to individuals, or the retail market. They leave that to the wholesalers.) The size of the publisher will dictate the size of the sales department. Some publishers have local sales reps that actually travel to individual stores and libraries with samples of the latest releases.

With a major bookstore, the publisher first must sell the national Barnes and Noble rep on carrying your title. Barnes and Noble then puts your book in their system, and includes your title in their in-house catalogue that goes to every Barnes and Noble listing the contact information of your distributor. From there, each store places individual orders based on their market. This is no guarantee that your book will reach the Barnes and Noble shelves, but it will be briefly promoted in the in-house catalogue. You also must be in the system before you can do an event at a Barnes and Noble.

When a Barnes and Noble (the wholesaler) in Memphis orders 10 copies of your book, the distributor sells them for 40% off retail, and the publisher and distributor split the 60% 45/15. That's $9.57 per book sale price: $1.44 goes to the distributor, leaving the publisher $8.13. You get 6% of that = $.49 per book.

Here's how the food chain works:
Publisher—sells to distributor for 55% off cover price;
Distributor—to wholesaler for 40% off cover price;
Wholesaler—to consumer for cover price.

The 10 books are shipped from the distributor's warehouse to the bookstore to sit on the shelf and wait to be bought. Bear in mind, in this day and age there are millions of books and only so much live bookshelf space. A friend of mine who publishes travel books with St. Martin's

Press tells me her publisher now has to *rent* space on the shelves of major bookstores.

So 5,000 copies of your book are sitting in a warehouse and, facing this fierce competition, you are now responsible for selling them. Part of your submission package was that comprehensive business plan of how you intended to sell your book. It's certainly not an impossible task, especially if it's a timely topic or you have the opportunity for mass exposure.

But aside from their relationships with bookstore chains and their catalog publications, unless you're Paris Hilton, Tiger Woods or Princess Di, publishers will expect you to hire a PR person to get you on media shows, talk radio interviews, local morning show appearances, anything to get you free air time to generate sales.

In the beginning, publishers might arrange for some book signings, but publishers are not PR agencies. At those events, the bookstore pays the publisher for what gets sold, and the publisher gives you your 6%.

You may also have to create your own events where you sell the books. A talk to the local chamber of commerce or your church group can sell books. You buy books from the publisher for a discount (make sure it's in the contract), creating a bigger profit margin than royalties. But you have to ship them to the location, or carry them with you, set up the display, handle the money, etc.

If you aren't constantly working to prove you are salable to your publisher (meaning, you have to sell books), it is very likely that your book will languish and eventually be shelved.

At that point, whatever is left of the 5,000 might be remaindered: sold off cheap in bulk to a remainder house who then sell them through catalogues or to Barnes and Noble for the Christmas sale racks. Or the publisher can do what is known as "pulping," an old-school term for recycling.

Pulping began after World War II when it was more cost effective to turn unsold books back into paper than ship them across the country. Bookstores would rip the covers off the books and send them back to the publisher as proof they'd been destroyed. The books were supposed to be burned or recycled. More often than not they'd end up in flea markets or used bookstores.

Today, it's more common to remainder books, but if these don't sell, they get recycled.

On top of all this, the publisher has the right to simply allow your book to go out of print forever.

Be aware that because of the cost and time required to get signed, then edit, design, print, and transport 5,000 books to the distributor and eventually and hopefully to the bookstore, the process of becoming a published author through a traditional publisher can take years and is costly. And after all that work, your publisher can just let it go out of print.

Often, but not always, will they offer you a chance to buy your rights back. I've heard of more than one story of the publisher pulping someone's inventory, either without giving the author a chance to buy the books back, or the author not being in a financial position to purchase the inventory.

Do It Yourself

These circumstances inspired me to self-publish. As much as I saw the value in having a big name publisher behind me, I hated the idea of my book being held hostage. I needed copies immediately to sell at my events, as well as on my new website. I sure as heck wasn't going to allow anyone to put my hard work on the shelf. And the thought of someone having the power to change my title gave me chills.

I learned the ins and outs of music publishing early in my career as a singer-songwriter. I had a musical partner once who released his own album (remember vinyl records?). He named his work "Heart Travels" and recorded ten beautiful love songs. The cover was a grainy black and white of him and me, nose to nose, taken by one of our dear friends. Many sales later, a record label in Chicago bought the rights to re-release it. They immediately changed the name to "Carousel Man" and re-shot the full-color cover with him on a merry-go-round. We joked later that the horse was in focus but he was not. And he couldn't do a thing about it.

As a musician, I was no stranger to self-promotion. At 17, I had a set of original songs I sang solo and played piano on; my first professional gig was right out of high school. As a performer, much of my job was on the phone booking the gigs with clubs and colleges, making the posters, sending out the mailings, hauling PA equipment and writing new music.

In the early 80s I began to catalog my songs. I needed recordings to send to the copyright office, and copies to sell from the stage. To save money in costly mixing and editing, I went guerrilla.

Laying out the order of the songs, I went into the studio and recorded them live to a cassette in that order. After I finished performing side one, I'd have the engineer flip the cassette, and record side two on the other side. This allowed me to take that master and do high-speed cassette duplications on my own double-sided boom box in my hotel room.

I designed all the cassette inserts freehand, using old fashioned typewriter copy, Xeroxes of photographs, hand-drawn art all stuck to the master page with spray cement and then photocopied and hand cut. The result was an obviously homemade product, but it got the job done. Today, looking back on those crudely manufactured works, they are more like art than design.

In 1987, I was contracted by a karate teacher to compose music for his classes. I had to design a cover and layout the cassette label. Apple computers were just beginning to be desktop, and a software called Pagemaker was the standard. This was a revolution in homegrown design. I locked myself in a room for two weeks with the instruction manual and the software and figured out how it worked. Using those new skills I designed the karate series, and life was never the same.

When it came time to make a website of my own, I did the same with a software program called Pagemill. Control of the website was a huge priority for me: to be able to make changes whenever I needed, quickly and cheaply. Because of this, I learned how to build websites and to this day maintain my own. For me, it's another form of expressing my muse of creativity, in the field of commerce.

Years later, when my coauthors and I hired a literary agent in New York City, I got an inside look at the book world. I found it strangely reminiscent of rock and roll. Not the character of publishing; that I found staid and conservative compared to the music industry. The promotion and public appearances necessary to sell books was very similar to gigging and selling CDs. But if the publisher is expecting me to do most of the work, why am I only getting 6%?

I realized the publisher was merely the sales system that would take my manuscript from final draft to bookstore then collect the money and distribute it accordingly. Period. Why couldn't I do that?

I could and did. For my first book, my coauthors and I created a business entity, Synergy Alliance, a small press, and followed Dan Poynter's *Self-Publishing Manual*, a highly comprehensive resource for approaching traditional self-publishing in 1997. I designed and laid out the initial book, then hired a designer for the cover and to put into proper graphic form for the printer. We decided on an initial print run of 1,000 books. I then began booking events around the country at bookstores, healing centers and churches. Meanwhile, our literary agent began sending out copies to major publishers.

The down side of being self-published at the time was that there was still a stigma with traditional publishing. By taking the initiative to publish my own book, ironically I was actually looked down upon by some major publishers.

This was due partly to a form of self-publishing that arose in the 1950s called "vanity press." These were publishers who you could pay to publish your book. There was no submission process, anyone with money could pay them to go through the steps to edit, design and manufacture a book. These publishers were not taken seriously by the "real" world of publishing, thus the moniker. It was considered a vanity to publish yourself, because you must be so vane to not understand how bad you are since you can't get signed with a "real" publisher. However, the practice of self-publishing has been around much longer than modern publishers would like to admit.

Stepping as far back as the late 1800s, authors were more often than not expected to pay for the printing of their work. In fact, many classics were originally self-published. The list of revered and respected writers who began as self-published is inspiring, including but not limited to Walt Whitman, Benjamin Franklin, Virginia Wolff, James Joyce, Mark Twain, ee cummings, Deepak Chopra, Carl Sandburg, George Bernard Shaw, and Upton Sinclair, to name a gracious few.

In the middle 20th century (pre-Internet) major publishers worked hand in hand with major distributors to provide bookstores and libraries with books to buy or borrow. The major distributors did not welcome self-published authors and bookstores bought their books from the major distributors. Bookstores simply could not deal with every individual author. Distributors eventually began to work with self-published authors, but only with a solid business plan. If you didn't sell enough to make them money, they would cancel the contract and send your books back to you. This made it nearly impossible for authors who self-published to get into the system.

At the time my first book came out in 1997, this system was failing. Publishers were paying big advances to "authors" whose names they thought could sell books, even if they weren't authors. Famous "non-authors"—Rue Paul, Shaquille O'Neal, Paris Hilton—were paid huge advances and had large print runs, only to find the books didn't sell. This meant sometimes hundreds of thousands of books sitting in a warehouse losing money. Meanwhile, it was becoming harder for an unknown to get in the door, as more and more people were submitting manuscripts, all the while the industry was downsizing.

To complicate matters, publishing's heritage was putting word to paper. The construction of a book was a sacred art; how could publishing come to grips with the digital age?

Great traditions were being challenged, and old school publishing went kicking and screaming. Meanwhile, those who saw the power of this animal called Internet began to find independent avenues to reach the buyers.

You can see the tremendous amount of waste in the traditional publishing process. Not only in bulk printing, shipping, selling and remaindering/recycling but in signing big names with big advances who don't sell. Many authors of true talent receive little or no advance and 2–3% royalties. Yes, that's 2-3% of sales. So if you were nobody, even if you had written the next great American novel, your chances of getting signed were slim to none.

As publishers had to cut costs, suddenly this old system started to crumble. By the time I attended Book Expo in New York City in 2007 to promote *Imagining Einstein*, the biggest and most reputable distributor in the industry, Publishers Group West (PGW), had just filed bankruptcy and all the new authors' books slated to arrive at the expo were being held hostage, taken into custody as part of PGW's assets. How proud was I to be there, my books in hand, while half the other attendees were SOL.

If you still think you want to get signed with a major publisher, go for it. However, with some technological savvy and a good plan, you can take an entirely different approach to publishing, one that is tailor-made for your needs and ambitions, resources and talents. You will keep 100% of the profits of all books sold, retain complete editorial, design, sales and manufacturing control, without pressure to sell and never a chance that your book will go out of print.

Today's technology allows the electronics of publishing to be readily available to everyone. With a laptop and the right software and skills, it's easier than ever to write, design and publish your own book. In fact, I run my entire empire from my laptop in bed. Every month, my distributor deposits my profit checks into my bank account while I sleep.

Perhaps the most revolutionary invention since the printing press that has allowed this new world of publishing to emerge is a process called Print-on-Demand.

Print-on-Demand (POD)

The old world of printing uses a process called offset lithography. Printing presses require plates that transfer the ink to a rubber surface and then onto large rolls of paper on which several books are printed. Once the sheets are printed they get dried, cut and bound, and are then shipped to a warehouse to be stored until sold.

The advantage of offset printing is that the more books printed, the cheaper the per-book cost. Since the plates and set-up are a large part of the cost, the bigger the print run the less expensive each book. The quality is high but the downside is the time required (weeks), as well as the infeasibility of printing a small run or even single books.

POD completely revolutionized the way books can be printed. Printing is done on a special machine that prints the insides and the cover, and then binds them all in one fell swoop. Like a Xerox machine for making books, it costs the same to print one book as it does to print 500,000. It does away with plates, print runs, shipping, and storing large quantities of books since you only print what you sell. This reduces recycling and allows for changing or editing the manuscript as you go.

Even though it costs the same to print one or 10,000, POD printers give volume discounts. In the end, it can wind up being just as cost effective for large orders then offset, not to mention the time and resources saved in the long run. From order to delivery is days with POD as opposed to months with offset.

In 1997, POD was a lovely idea whose time had not yet come. So my coauthors and I used offset to print 1,000 copies of our book, divided the inventory up between the three of us to store in our basements and attics, and sell at our events and off the Internet. Synergy Alliance handled the business.

Back then, it took months of designing and meetings with the printer, waiting to get into the printing queue. But when the boxes finally arrived, we were spinning. Holding those books in our hands was priceless, especially after four years of work.

I learned the major bookstores would not stock our book until we were carried through a major distributor. We happened to have one in our city, and after many hoops, we landed an account with them. This allowed me to submit requests to Barnes and Noble, Borders, Walden Books and others to be included in their systems.

I also targeted local bookstores, as area authors are a big draw even in major chains. I launched a small release as we traveled around the country, talking at bookstores, churches, metaphysical shops, and anywhere else we could about our story, all the while selling our book.

For my second book, *Party of Twelve: The Afterlife Interviews*, it only made sense to use what I learned from the first one to expand my platform. In 2001, I broke away from my partners and started my own publishing company so I could keep the rights, design, editorial, project management control as well as all the profits. POD still was not perfected, so I used a printer on the East Coast and stored the books in my attic.

By the time *Einstein* was released in 2007, POD was a hair's breathe from being full-blown. Only the most savvy of book publishing aficionados understood what was happening, but it was happening. A company called Lightning Source Inc. (LSI) was about to explode on the scene and completely change the way not only printing, but sales and distribution were handled.

For this release, I hired a company out of St. Louis to help me promote. I wanted to go worldwide and found an organization named IFP Enterprises that specialized in helping small presses promote their works. After two trips to Missouri to meet and negotiate with the two women who started the business, we were up and running, preparing for a release date of April 17, 2007 in Princeton, New Jersey. IFP would take care of booking events, sales, promotion, fulfillment, website presence, and public relations in exchange for 20% and $1,000 a month. It was going to be perfect!

At their urging, we printed 3,000 books offset, paying $1.50 a book. The 3,000 were shipped to St. Louis (about $800), where the team would be fulfilling orders while I was on the road speaking and signing. They were working on a website, had sent out sell cards, and began booking events around the country. We had weekly phone meetings beginning in January to prepare to launch on the anniversary of Einstein's death in the town he last lived.

IFP also entered me in the IPPY book award contest, conducted annually by the Independent Publisher Book Awards to honor the year's best independently published titles. IPPYs were being awarded at Book Expo America, the biggest book convention in the world, taking place in New York City that June, where they were planning on having a booth. Much to my amazement and joy, I won in the category of Fiction: New Age!

I booked my plane tickets for Princeton, made arrangements to stay with a friend on the East Coast, and prepared to begin my journey to superstardom. IFP had gotten me three events that April, one at a bookstore in the Village in New York City, and I couldn't have been more excited.

The night before I left, as I packed my suitcase, I received a phone call from my partner. She regretted to inform me, she said, that they were going out of business, and should she ship the 3,000 books to my home in Corpus Christi?

One can only imagine the panic that ensued. After the shock wore off, I got to work. I arranged to have the books shipped to a friend's home in Oregon (another $800), where she had a barn, and lots of time to help fulfill orders. I continued to show up at events they had booked, including Book Expo, where I met the wonderful salespeople from Lightning Source, who finally brought me into the 21st century. In the end, it was a blessing in disguise.

The New Publishing

Print-on-Demand has finally grown up. (If I had only known before I printed 3,000 books.) Technology caught up with necessity, and LSI can not only print one book at a time cost-effectively ($2.88 for *Imagining Einstein*) but is the distributor as well. They oversee all my sales portals, including online bookstores all over the world, like Barnesandnoble.com/Italy and Amazon.com/Germany. LSI puts up the pages and customers who order from those sites receive the book directly from LSI, who prints and ships. No warehouse, no storage, no excess. We only print what we sell. At the end of the month, LSI puts money into my bank account while I sleep. I keep 100% of the profits.

Let's revisit shopping our manuscript to traditional publishers. In our meeting with the commissioning editors, we agreed to 6% royalty and to a first print run of 5,000 books that retail at $15.95.

If all 5,000 books sold for retail, total profits could round up to $80,000. Of that, you would receive $4800 ($15.95 x 5,000 = $79,750 x .06 = $4785). That leaves $75,000. 55% of this goes to the distributor, which is about $41,000, leaving $34,000 going to the publisher. The cost of printing the book might have been about $2 each, and shipping the original print run to the distributor adds another $.50 a book. This leaves $21,500, which pays the editor, designer, sales person and all the execs at the publishing company.

In truth, no print run sells 100% at retail price. You can purchase books from the publisher at a discount and sell them retail at events. Even a bookstore book signing has 40% going to the bookstore. It's not realistic to think you can gross $80,000 for 5,000 books as a self-publisher. Let's look at the numbers in Guerrilla Publishing.

Let's say you want to sell 5000 books. Here are some possible scenarios for our guerrilla approach:

One thousand books you purchase at cost ($3) from your POD printer/distributor and sell for full retail price $15.95 at events you host. $15,950 - $3,000 (printing) = $12,950.

Two thousand sell on Internet bookstore sites. LSI takes 55% as distributor, and minus the cost of the book is your profit. 2000 x $15.95 = $31,900 – $17,545 (55%) = $14,355 - $6,000 (printing) = $8355.

Two thousand you sell at book signings hosted by local and major chain bookstores. You purchase the books at cost and bring them with you. The bookstore sells them for retail price and takes 40%. 2000 x $15.95 = $31,900 - $12,760 (40%) = $19,140 - $6,000 (printing) = $13,140.

All told you make $34,445. Deduct the approximately $1500 it took to create your system, and your final tally is

$32,945. In the old world, you made $4800 and still had to do the same amount of promotion and sales work. Really.

Follow me as I show you my publishing empire, run from my laptop in my bedroom or from any hotel room anywhere in the world. See how easy it is to be not only a published author but a publisher as well.

CHAPTER FIVE: The Project Matrix

Back when we were learning to live the life of an author, we identified our needs and our resources, and rearranged our lives to accommodate the intention to become published. Here we engage in a similar process to create a project matrix that will identify the team we need to build and the tasks that need to be accomplished in order to complete this job of publishing the book.

With you at the helm as project manager, you begin by identifying which roles need to be filled and what are the responsibilities of those roles. Remember, these are *not* your partners. You are the boss. You are hiring these people to fulfill your wishes when it comes to editorial content, design, sales, and distribution. So while you want their expert advice and a good working relationship, in the end, you are the CEO and they are your freelancers.

Let's look at all the roles and responsibilities you will need to fill to get your book up and out into the world. Remember, we are making a list of your needs, and then will look at your resources to see how and where we can fill them.

Project Management

Before anything, you must accept responsibility for being the leader of managing the project of getting your manuscript into printed form and out into the world. This is perhaps the most important position of all. As we discussed in the writing section, you can write until the cows come home, but until you manage the project—put it on paper, lay it out into a book, and have it printed—you are not a published author.

Large corporations often hire people specifically trained to manage large, complex projects. They have degrees in project management and computer software that tracks every detail—resources, needs, team, timelines—necessary to complete the project within the deadline. You, too, could hire someone to implement your project, but you are still ultimately in charge of moving it along to fruition.

To create your project management matrix, fill in the following information:

Mission Statement

Here is where you articulate the biggest vision possible of what you are trying to accomplish in one small statement. Consider it a self-imposed "big picture" commitment that serves as inspiration to accomplish a goal. In this case, your mission statement could be, "To become a published author by publishing the book, "INSERT TITLE HERE." You could add things like, "and be sustained living the life of an author" if you are inspired.

Now everything concerning this project is held up against this statement. Does this decision serve to advance that mission?

For example, you are writing a book about Christianity called, "What If Jesus Were Here Now?" One of your friends mentions your book to their pastor. The pastor calls and asks if you would like to speak about your work at the Tuesday night church book club. Does saying yes to this invitation advance your mission to become a published author of that book? Yes, certainly. You are expanding your network, gaining future readers, learning more about your subject and practicing your public speaking skills.

However, one of the attendees has started writing a book researching the lost books of the bible and asks you if you want to partner with them. It is the same field, after all. So you ask, would this advance your mission to publish your book? No. It might help you become a published author, but not of the work that is the focus of your mission statement.

In this way your mission statement keeps you clearly on track in your decision-making process.

The Team

Identify the people you need in your team. Even if you don't know any designers, someone will have to perform that task. List all the players needed to complete the mission. You can find people to fulfill them as you go.

> **Project Sponsor:** The person who initiates the project and ultimately has the final say. This is you.
>
> **Project Manager:** The one in charge of holding team members accountable for their part of the project and in the timeframe allotted. More than likely, you, but could be someone else.
>
> **Team Members:** The rest of the team has buy-in to the specific functions assigned to them. Here are the major players:

> **Author(s)**
> You have hopefully already finished your manuscript but if you haven't, finding a coauthor can be a blessing and a curse. There is something to be said for collaboration, but often times we end up in partnership only because we don't believe we can do it ourselves. We think we need someone else to move us along. This dynamic breeds resentment and makes collaboration more difficult.

Make sure you actually need a coauthor before you commit. Writing together is an art; trust your own talents and honor your own voice.

Editors
I am a huge believer in self-editing. I spend more hours editing my work than I do writing it. However, there comes a time when it is mandatory to have at least three sets of eyes to scrutinize your work.

Find people for your resource list that would be willing to read your manuscript and tell you what they think, like a content editor. Friends and family will often enjoy looking over your work and giving you their thoughts. People find typos and tense errors, and the more feedback you receive of your work the better.

Ask them to tell you if the story makes sense, if the characters are believable, if the plot flows, if you left anything out. Any and all feedback is appreciated.

Then take what they say, and consider it for yourself. In the end, you have final say. Don't be overwhelmed thinking you have to make every change everyone suggests. Consider the feedback, and do what feels right for you.

After you've had everyone from your pastor to Grandma Martha read it and you've incorporated the appropriate content changes, hire a good copy editor, no matter what. You should be able to get a good one for about $300 depending on how long your book is. This last edit and proof is worth spending money on.

When you are through incorporating these changes, proof it one last time and call it done.

Designer

If you have any graphic design skills or experience, consider learning to lay out the book yourself. I cannot say enough about taking the time to learn these skills, as they will serve you for the rest of your life. If I counted up all the money I saved over the years doing my own book layouts, flyers and website, I bet even I would be surprised.

These days you can lay out a book in Microsoft Word. In the end, if design just isn't your strength, plan to pay anywhere from $1 to $3 a page.

Contact graphic design departments of local trade schools to find students who would do your project for an affordable price. Ask in your networks, or go to Craig's List under "services:writing." Google "book designers" and do some research. Better yet, get the software and take a class, using your book as your first learning project. The skills you pick up here will serve you for years to come.

Go to the library or bookstore and look at book designs. Search Amazon.com for books of your genre and look at their covers. Often you can preview the insides of the book. Notice the typeface, layout styles, page numbers, headers and footers and anything else that strikes you. Start to formulate an idea of what you want your design to look like.

Notice the difference between design styles from a major publisher and books that are self-published or from a small press. Traditional publishers tend to use more "serif" fonts like Times New Roman or my favorite, calisto 11 point with 14 point leading (the space between the lines). Self-published books sometimes use "san serif" fonts like verdana or helvetica.

There is a science to the title page and the credits, as I call them. This is where all the vital statistics are listed, including copyright, ISBN and LCCN numbers, which we will get into later.

Your printer will have templates that will allow you or your designer to easily know the exact measurements and how wide to make the spine. Be sure to leave enough room in the margins for note takers. Since I am not one, I made the mistake of having tiny margins without realizing the aggravation it would cause some of my readers.

Do you have any friends who are artists? Would they be willing to give you the right to reprint their artwork on your cover? If so, be sure to give them credit on the title page.

Remember, using OPA (other people's artwork) will require permission from the artists, including the photographer of a picture. And don't be fooled into thinking if it's on the Internet, it's free. There are websites that sell clip art and stock photographs, and others that license the work to you.

When I was designing the cover of *Einstein*, I wanted to use a famous picture of Albert Einstein sticking out his tongue, but the cost was prohibitive. I ended up using a piece of clip art of a compass that I had in my files, blew it up and faded it out.

Party of Twelve: The Afterlife Interviews was a design rip-off from the first *Catcher in the Rye* edition, a deep red cover with gold lettering and nothing but the title and author.

Traditionally, the back cover has quotes from the book, review lines from notable people and often a picture of the author. I prefer nothing on the back. I put my author information, including picture, bio and highlights of my other works on the inside back pages. Why? No reason other than I can. I like the clean look of an uninterrupted back cover. I still try to keep a look of a major publisher, using elegant fonts and tasteful cover art, but the point is, you can do anything your heart desires because you are in charge.

Webmaster

If you have published your book for friends and family, with no intention to sell, then you don't need a website. If you want to sell your book from your own portal and become a retailer, you will need a web presence, and one of your team members should be a webmaster.

Today, it's easier than ever to build and maintain a one-page website for little or no cost. In fact, your print-on-demand printer might include one in the deal, or allow you to build your own storefront.

Web building software is more affordable and easier than ever to use. Webmasters abound, so if you need one, do your research and find one that fits your budget, will be responsive to your immediate needs and does work you like.

Print-on-Demand/Distributor

There are numerous options when it comes to selecting a print-on-demand printer who also distributes your books worldwide. Google "Print on Demand" and you will find Booksurge, Lulu, Xlibris, and CafePress to name a few. It's important to pick one that works for you.

Stay away from "online publishers" who claim for $199 they can make you a published author. Read all the fine print; sometimes that price is only the beginning. Cover design, marketing, and editorial services all are extras. You end up paying more for something you could create ala carte on your own and get 100% of the profits.

However, if you are not interested in doing this yourself and wish to find a full-service POD who also offers editing, design and marketing services, and price is no object, Outskirts is a reputable company, but it will cost you. Plus, the "marketing" section has resources that they have compiled for you to do it yourself. An actual marketing service, such as Outskirts sending out press releases, will be extra.

After extensive research into available print-on-demand companies, I found Lightning Source Inc. and Lulu.com to be the best match for me.

Ingram, one of the largest traditional distributors in the world, owns Lightning Source Inc. With printing plants in Tennessee and the UK, and even more distribution centers, LSI prints on demand and fulfills around the world. Offering a $12 a year per book global distribution package, LSI will create sales web pages on all major online bookstores around the world and handle all aspects of sales and distribution to all wholesalers. They don't do retail.

However you can drop ship your retail sales (meaning you place the order yourself with Lightening Source, and they send it directly to your customer with your company as the return address and charge you the cost of printing, shipping and handling). You can also drop ship special orders from bookstores.

The application process for LSI is rigorous but worth the time. There is a charge to upload electronic files of about $79, but the cost per book is much less than any other I have found. Every spring they have a free upload sale as well.

They also provide an extensive library of templates, worksheets and design tools, and assign a real live customer service rep available to assist in all areas. There is an extra charge to upload a new edition of the same manuscript.

What they don't offer is add-on services of press releases, editing, design, etc. They focus on printing and worldwide distribution only, and the cost of the book reflects that efficiency.

Lulu.com comes in a close second, but for other purposes. Lulu offers a sales presence: an online retail storefront to personalize and use as your website, or that can be linked up to become the shopping cart portion of your website.

Unlike Lightning Source, who will not provide you with a retail storefront of your own, Lulu has easy-to-use storefront templates and styles, and makes it fun to create your sales presence. If you don't have another website, this is a great way to have one to sell your book. When someone orders a copy, Lulu prints, ships, collects the money, and puts it in your bank account while you sleep, once a month.

Lulu does not charge for uploading the graphics of the book or revisions. However the cost per book is significantly more than Lightning Source and you only get 80% of the profits. This makes it a great place to shape your book before uploading the final to LSI.

For example, I first published this book you are reading on Lulu in a short run of ten. Lulu allows the option to keep your work private or make it available for publication. I kept it private, printed the short run and asked my initial readers to proof it in exchange for the free copy. This meant even more sets of eyes proofing it before loading the final version up to Lightning Source and into the system—fini!

The final version at Lulu also goes public and enters into the Lulu.com general shopping system. If you were to go to Lulu you could order my books, but since I don't direct anyone to it, I rarely sell there. I prefer my own website and use Paypal as my shopping cart, which is covered later on.

Both companies offer "international distribution." This means they set up your sales pages on Amazon.com, barnesandnoble.com, etc. all over the world. When someone buys a book there, the order goes directly to the distributor to be fulfilled.

My designated distributor was Lightning Source, who set up all the pages and manages them for a cost of $12 a year. However, Lulu decided to instigate their free distribution program without asking me. They set up duplicate pages on Amazon.com, et al. This meant Lulu's webpage overrode LSI's and orders went to Lulu, which charged significantly more to print. I had to specifically write to Lulu and tell them to cease and desist. Be aware of this if you are going to use both.

One of the greatest innovations of print-on-demand is the ability to print short runs in the beginning and having a period of continual refinement of your book. I highly recommend using these two POD/distributors as a part of your entire system.

Event Planner

Having been a musician for many years, I was accustomed to booking gigs. Instead of calling a club or college to convince them to hire me to play music, I call bookstores and convince them to host a book signing. Since bookstores are always looking for authors, you'd be surprised how easy it is to arrange.

Whether you decide to book these gigs yourself, or contract it out, this is the easiest and most cost effective way to sell books: at an event where people are present because of you and your book. Someone must take charge of making this happen.

Goals

Now that you have your team identified, you create goals. Goals are measurable outcomes that will lead to the fulfillment of the mission. This is where we get more specific.

Remember, goals must be *measurable*. They must have details that can be identified so you will clearly see when you have reached one: your book is in your hand; a website is up and running; money is in the bank. So articulate your goals: to finish the manuscript, get it into book form and available for purchase. Be sure to speculate on a time frame. You can always change it, but put an end point in sight.

Goals should be realistic and doable. They need to fit in your schedule and you must have the resources to accomplish them or be willing to find them. Articulating them clearly is the first step to bring them into reality.

Objectives

Objectives are the measurable steps you are going to take to accomplish your goals. This is where you begin to break down the details of the plan. List each goal and then the steps you will take to make it happen. Finishing your manuscript may require the objectives of watching less television, working more on the book, contacting Aunt Helen to watch the kids Tuesday morning, or conducting a needs assessment for where you are in the process. Getting it into book form may require objectives to find a designer, research other cover art and layout, or find a printer.

Tasks and Timeline

List all the tasks involved in accomplishing the objectives and the timeline for when it should be complete. In this way you leave no stone unturned in your mission to become the author of a published work entitled, "INSERT TITLE HERE." Your project matrix should look something like this:

Mission: To become the published author of *How To Become A Published Author For Less Than $1500 & Keep 100% Of The Profits* by October 30, 2010

Team:
Project Sponsor & Manager: Barbara With
Author: Barbara With
Editors: Barbara With, Cathy Kline, Debbie Reinertson
Designers: Barbara With, Holly Adams
Printers/Distributors: Lightning Source and Lulu.com
Webmaster: Barbara With
Event Planner: Barbara With and local city co-hosts TBD

Goals:
- ❑ Finish manuscript
- ❑ Design and print book
- ❑ Get into the distribution system and create website
- ❑ Book 10 events and sell 500 books by end of year

Objectives:
- Decide on designer
- Finalize design
- Finalize website
- Upload graphics to printer
- Order 100 copies
- Contact bookstores and book events
- Research PR opportunities

Tasks:
- Contact Joe's brother Bill, the designer
- Call the community college graphic design department, interview possible designers
- Ask Sarah who she used for her brochures
- Choose designer and finalize design: September 30
- Proof designs and send proofs back to designer
- Incorporate changes and upload finals to Lulu.com: October 2
- Order test copies and proof
- Incorporate changes and upload to Lightning Source by October 15
- Google local bookstores and gather phone numbers
- Decide which bookstores to target
- Conduct telephone campaign to book events
- Prepare presentation for book signings by October 30
- Book travel arrangements
- Go do the first book signing October 30

When you are done, you have a plan to work from, to keep yourself on track, to know where you are. Nothing is set in stone; the great part about being your own publisher, you can change release dates. I kept pushing out the release date for *Party of Twelve: Post 9/11*, having underestimated the amount of time my straight job would take up while I was writing. No problem!

With this plan, let's get into the brass tacks of the job, what I call the Vital Statistics.

CHAPTER SIX: Vital Statistics

In the publishing industry, there are specific numbers, registrations and affiliations that you need to make in order to put your book into the system to be sold worldwide. What follows is specific information needed to accomplish this goal.

ISBN, Bowker and Books in Print

In 1879, Bowker became the first agency to officially issue identifying numbers and a catalog for all books in print. Short for *International Standard Book Number*, this 13-digit number is assigned by Bowker to identify every book that gets published. *Books in Print* is the industry standard, the master list of every book that has ever been assigned an ISBN.

In the old days, Bowker would publish a multiple-volume edition twice a year that would get shipped to libraries and bookstores. When the digital age descended, they put the catalog on a set of CD-ROMs and shipped once a month. Today, *Books in Print* is online, available free and 24 hours a day. Here's how it works.

You as the publisher buy an ISBN number from Bowker for about $200 (they are cheaper by bulk but you can obtain a single number for about this price). Then at Bowkerlink.com you register your publisher information, as well as assigning the ISBN to your book title. Once you have registered, you are automatically included in *Books in Print* Online. There is no cost for this. Done. Now anyone can find your book. Forever.

Quite literally, assignment of ISBN is forever. Once you have declared a book associated with a number in Bowker, you cannot use that ISBN for any other product. If for any reason you decide not to sell your book and don't care if anyone can find it, you still cannot assign that ISBN to another book.

You will be asked to provide detailed information about your book and your company: names, titles, numbers, contact information, and any information related to your small press, but most importantly, your distributor. Now, any time anyone goes into any bookstore in the United States, they can ask the clerk to look up your book in *Books in Print* and special order it.

In my case, when a fan in Michigan goes into the Detroit Barnes and Noble and special orders *Imagining Einstein*, Barnes and Noble goes online to *Books In Print* to discover they need to place the order directly with Lightning Source. The customer pays Barnes and Noble, who then pays LSI, who then prints and ships to Michigan (even directly to the buyer's home) and deposits my money into my account at the end of the month. Because Ingram, one of the biggest traditional book distributors in the world, owns LSI, I know my books will be paid for and delivered, and I will get my money. We've come a long way from the stigma of "vanity press."

For me, special orders are a sufficient and easy way to make my books available through storefront bookstores. I have no interest in competing with millions of other books for the right to sit on the shelf and may be bought. Unpurchased books get returned or, if they can't be returned, they are destroyed. Either way, if you've sold Barnes and Noble on buying copies of your book to sit on their shelves and they don't sell, you owe the Barnes and Noble a refund. Technicaly you decide if you will refund or not and list it in your Bowker information. A bookstore might balk at buying it if they don't think they can return it. B&N demands it or they won't work with you. However, when a customer specifically wants to order the book, the risk of a return is lower.

You can aslo send your book, along with the application found on the Barnes and Noble website, to their small press division to get entered into the Barnes and Noble system. This will qualify you for holding events at all Barnes and Noble stores.

Trade Discounts

Your Bowkerlink account will also ask to create what is called a *trade discount*: the percentage off your retail price that the wholesaler or distributor pays the publisher for your book. The greater the trade discount, the more money there is to split up among the parties involved in selling your book.

Typically, distributors get 55% off retail and wholesalers (bookstores) get 40% off. You determine the price and the structure of the discounts. Once you decide, you enter that information into your Bowker account so wholesalers will know their price. You then give that information to your distributor who sells your books at the price you request.

Again, Barnes and Noble won't take less than 40% off. As big dogs, they can call their own shots. But other independent bookstores are more willing to work with lesser discounts.

LCCN

Short for *Library of Congress Control Number*, an LCCN helps facilitate distribution through the United States library system and also includes the submission of your book to the Library of Congress after publication. It is also referred to as a PCN, or *Preassigned Control Number*. Go to http://pcn.loc.gov/ and apply for one for your book. It's free.

This is a two-step process: ordering the LCCN number, and then once the book has been printed, shipping one to the Library of Congress.

Never pay anyone more than a small administrative fee to obtain an LCCN number for you. They are free and applying for one is as easy as filling out a form. Outskirts Press will charge you $99!

EAN Bar Code

Short for *European Article Number*, this is also referred to as the IAN for *International Article Number* and is the international barcode standard. This graphic is used as a reference key to look up information about the product line held on a database. Merchants enter your barcode data into their systems, and then have the ability to scan the code when they sell your book.

There are numerous online services that offer instant purchase and same-day service of the graphics for your personal barcode. You provide the ISBN and the price, and they create the graphic that your designer puts onto the back cover of the book. Average price is about $15.

If you don't plan to market your book, the barcode is not necessary. But if you want to sell it anywhere other than your own events, a barcode is mandatory.

Copyright

The US Office of Copyrights was established to provide protection to people who create what is referred to as "original works of authorship" in the United States. This protection is extended to both published and unpublished works. A copyright gives you the legal right to exclusively distribute, sell, reproduce, display, and/or perform your works, and makes it illegal for anyone else to do that without permission.

Copyright is granted to a specific expression of your work. In other words, you cannot copyright an idea. You are copyrighting a tangible and measurable form of expression. For example, the idea of forming a "psychic sorority" cannot be copyrighted, but the book, "Diaries of a Psychic Sorority" can be. This does not guarantee you the rights to the term "psychic sorority"; that would be a trademark or register mark, which is a different and more expensive process requiring a lawyer to do a lengthy legal search and then register the trademark with the US Patent and Trademark office.

Similarly, a choreographed dance cannot be copyrighted, but a video of it can be. An improvisational speech cannot be registered, but a transcript of it can be. It is the actual physical articulation, word for word, that is copyright. This is the measure to see if someone copied you.

Copyright protects your book from others publishing it without your permission and is registered with the Library of Congress. It is as simple as filling out the form, and sending a copy of the book along with your check to the LOC.

Copyright will last for your lifetime plus 70 years past your death, when the work becomes public domain. This means it is now unprotected and anyone can publish it. *The Science of Getting Rich* by Wallace Waddell is an example of public domain. Anyone can reprint it, so I designed an e-book of it and offer it as a free download. Conveniently, I advertise my books, workshops and music in the back. This is classic Guerrilla Publishing.

The cost of filing for copyright, as of August 1, 2009 is $35 and can be done online at http://www.copyright.gov.

Web Hosts and Domain Names

When I built my first website in 1999, I did extensive research into the options of where to park it. All those years ago, selection was limited compared to what you can access today. Back then, Siteworks appealed to me not only because of the design of their website, cost, and friendliness, but they lived up to their tagline, "Service is our strength." I pay a little over $13 a month, and when the going gets tough, I can have a live human in the United States on the phone helping me through.

The President and I once emailed each other throughout the only interruption of service I've ever had in all these years. She was mortified that the servers were down and I gave her some support, since my site was not commerce-heavy. She was so appreciative. In all the years I have been with them, they have always exceeded my expectations and I have no intention of leaving them any time soon. Other companies can give you more for less as far as offerings and space, but if you want the best customer service available, I highly recommend Siteworks.

There are two kinds of website hosting: a site-building host, and a host that basically rents you server space to park the site you already built. The difference is, site-building hosts such as GoDaddy are basically providing you with their software to build your website that is parked on their server. Server renters such as Siteworks expect that you own the software and build your website on your own computer first, and then upload that to the server.

The downside of site-building hosts is that they don't allow you to take your site with you should you decide to move elsewhere. This is because building a website is like building a little city. There are folders for pictures, another for the pages themselves, others have different kinds of plug ins, etc. All the pages of the website are linked in a very specific way in order for it to load the same way on all computers. So, yes, you can walk away from GoDaddy with the basic pages, all the artwork, but not the structure. You need the website building software to reconstruct the structure of the site. My point is, why not just learn how to build one, or hire someone to build you one that is transferable.

Learning the basics of web page building will allow you to make changes as you need them, save money, and keep the entire site intact should you want to change service providers. I use GoLive, a part of Adobe InDesign package. But website building software is very affordable and you don't need tons of bells and whistles to make a basic site as a calling card with a Paypal button for your book.

Domain Names

To find out if the name you want for your website is taken, go to www.whois.net and plug it in. Once you find one that is available, you must find a service that will register the information about the website address. Your website host will have the official address numbers to give Registar. They will keep your address on file and remind you when it's time to re-register.

There are other domain registration companies, but Registar is one of the oldest and most reputable around.

It costs $49 for two years, or $149 for ten years. Other site-building hosts offer domain names for very cheap, but double check if it's because they must be parked on their site. Registar also has site-building software, and offers 7 gig of server space, unlimited email accounts and more, with domain registration.

Regardless if you wish to use Registar, you must find a domain registration company to assign your new address to your new domain name. That way, whoever types www.barbarawith.com wherever they are will come to the same place.

Shopping Carts

Somehow, you must have a way to accept payment for the sale of your book online. My advice is: the simpler the better. If you don't plan to do much e-business, such as promotions or collecting and tracking sales leads, set up a page that will work basically as your billboard and international cash register. Your Lulu.com storefront would work perfectly. No need to even buy a domain name.

However, if you are building from scratch, site hosts like GoDaddy include add-ons such as shopping carts, web stat analysis, and other business tools. Carefully consider what you need and make sure you factor in the costs of the add-ons.

Merchant accounts give you the ability to accept credit cards, but unless you plan to do large volumes, the cost and risk of establishing a merchant account, for me, was too great. All the extra hidden service fees and contracts were prohibitive. And what about the months I might not sell anything? I would still be paying for the account.

My pick for the fastest, easiest, safest solution is Paypal. Internationally known and respected, Paypal was one of the first companies that offered secure transactions over the Internet and charge per transaction.

After you open a Paypal account, they deposit two small sums of money into the bank account you indicate. Paypal will verify the account after you report back what sums were deposited.

To create a shopping cart, go to their easy-to-use Merchant Tools section, plug in the statistics of your product or service, and receive the code to paste into the website that produces the BUY NOW or ADD TO CART button people will click to buy your book. They will be directed to your product's information, and be asked to sign in or create a Paypal account of their own, and pay with a credit card.

Once a customer buys your book, Paypal sends you an email confirming you just made money, of which Paypal keeps about 3%. The email has all the information for fulfilling the order. When you log onto Paypal, you click on the order, click to print the shipping label complete with postage (know the weight of your book to calculate shipping). Then tape the shipping label on the front of a padded envelope in which you place the autographed copy of your book, and drop in a mailbox.

You have now just become a fulfillment house.

This method works as long as you are keeping website sales manageable and can handle fulfilling orders in your office or basement. If and when you become so successful that you are in demand as a speaker and on the road selling your book, there are other ways to cover sales at your website:

- ✓ Hire an out of work friend to monitor sales and fulfill orders.
- ✓ Drop ship from LSI.
- ✓ Instead of using Paypal, link sales directly to your Amazon.com page. You won't be receiving full retail price, but you will also not have to spend time fulfilling. Either way you will still make money in your sleep and keep 100% of your profits.

The Structure of Your Business

The beauty of the structure of your business in Guerrilla Publishing is that you can remain a sole proprietor. You don't have to register as a business entity. If you link your website to a wholesaler like Amazon or Lulu.com, they pay the sales tax. Since you are not doing the selling, you do not need a tax certificate. The revenue you receive is considered royalties and is taxed as income.

If you plan to sell books on your website, you will be considered a retailer, and have some tax considerations. If you plan to do business under a name other than your own, you must file a "Doing Business As" statement. Call your local paper and ask them specifically about this. They will take your information and print it in a special section of the want ads, then send you a copy when they publish it. You might need this if you wish to open a business checking account.

You will need a business address. If you rent a postal box, remember that mailbox facilities will not forward your mail should you change your address.

Instead of getting a business phone line, consider having a second number for your line with a different ring. This will let you know it's a business call. Or check into your cell service to see what the cost of another line is that you can dedicate just for business.

You will need to register with your state to pay sales tax. As a home-based business, you might run up against some zoning issues if your address is a residential zone. It could be as simple as an addendum assuring that your business does not involve customers coming to your premises.

Open a business bank account if you have a business name. Otherwise, just let LSI deposit your paychecks into your personal account at the end of each month.

As with any business revenue, keep records for tax time. Sole Proprietors file a Schedule C. If you have not been a freelancer before, educate yourself on what expenses can be deducted.

So. Here you are, your book in hand, online sales portals all over the world, perhaps several book signings coming up at some local bookstores. Now you are living the life of a published author. Congratulations! You have just accomplished one of your wildest dreams coming true. Woo hoo!

So how can you live this life full-time? Let me share the tips that have allowed me to travel the world, speaking and conducting workshops, selling books and getting paid to be a published author. Hopefully, it will help you begin to think outside the box and ideate a path for sustaining the fulfillment of your dream.

The truth is, even if you never do a book signing, if you have a book, you are officially a published author. Don't ever let that fact get lost. It's a huge accomplishment.

PART THREE:
Selling

CHAPTER SEVEN: Oprah

I was once on Oprah. No, not for my book. A nonprofit I worked for, WomenVenture, won an Angel Award. We were flown to Chicago to pick up that big $100,000 check. My boss, Tene, appeared on stage to get it, but there were several shots of me in the peanut gallery applauding and secretly reveling in the fact that it was my media contact that got us there.

Getting on Oprah is everyone's favorite fantasy. How I got us there was a strange set of circumstances that I had little to do with except being in the right place at the right time. This is the first lesson in selling yourself: opportunities come when you least expect them, so pay attention and be ready! You never know who will read your book and who they will pass it along to.

At the time of Oprah, I volunteered at the Portage for Youth, an after-school center in St. Paul, teaching songwriting and performing. The executive director's daughter went to the Oprah website and nominated her mother, Raeanne, for an Angel Award. Lo and behold, she received a call from the producer wanting to know more.

Raeanne was terrified of the media and often sent me in to be the spokesperson. She gave me the producer's phone numbers, which strangely included her home, and told me to follow up. The long and short was, that program was not selected to get the award, but I had the numbers for a producer at Oprah!

I hoarded those numbers, thinking I would use them when it came time to promote my book. However, one day Tene asked me to send out an email to the WomenVenture

Board of Directors asking if anyone had contacts with Oprah. Oprah was to be the keynote at a conference in Boston Tene was attending, and she thought if she had a contact, she could arrange to meet with Oprah while she was there.

I balked; this was my contact! Did I want to give it up to my company instead of using it for my own promotion? After a good long talk with myself, I decided to cough it up and gave it to Tene. We composed a beautiful letter about our organization and sent it to Chicago with our press package asking for an audience with Oprah, and off Tene went to Boston.

Needless to say, she returned with her tail between her legs. "What was I thinking?" she mused, "No one gets within a half a mile of Oprah unless Oprah says. We had to go through a metal detector, and I had nose bleed seats."

However, a week later, she received a call from the producer! I was in the office when she took the call. Her face contorted as she silently mouthed, "Oh my god it's *Oprah* on the phone!" while pointing at the receiver.

After listening in silence for a good while, I heard her say, "What would we do with the $100,000? Use it for a new program on financial literacy."

What I did not know was, Oprah had two different production teams: one for the show, and one for the Angel Awards segments. Rarely did the two meet. We sent our materials to the Angel Award producer, not the regular one. We thought we were asking for an audience with Oprah in Boston; she thought we were applying for an Angel Award! We had no idea! We accidentally won the award!

At that point, all hell broke loose at the office. Everything stopped for Oprah.

Next came the rigorous selection process to choose the clients who would be featured in the segment. Imagine asking a struggling female business owner if she would like to be featured on Oprah! Now imagine telling her a day later that she didn't make the cut. It was brutal.

The entire organization was thrown upside down because of this award. There were security checks, and at least 25 women were interviewed before they decided on three. Then came the day-long film shoot with the producers driving from one client location to the next, filming as the officers of the Board followed along like groupies.

As executive to the president, I organized all the details, including travel to Chicago. A limo picked us up and took us to the Omni Hotel on Chicago's famed Miracle Mile where we checked into our suites. The next day was spent in the studio, behind the scenes of both Harpo and the Angel Award foundation.

In the studio, I was seated on the end of the front row near the hallway where Oprah walks in and out. On the way out after the taping, I was right behind her. "You have made my life a living hell," I said behind her as we walked.

She turned, grabbed my hand, looked me in the eye and responded, "I love when I do that…"

I am zero degrees of separation from Oprah. How cool is that? The moral of the story is: you can't create synchronicity, but you can expect it to be a part of the process. Anything can happen at any time, like me on Oprah. It was dumb luck that got me there. No amount of planning could have accomplished that end. Even though going to the show wasn't for my book, someday I may very well have a chance to meet Oprah again as an author, and I will have a connection to reference to make myself stand out.

Having a marketing plan is great, but make your identity being a published author. Talk about yourself to others as a way to naturally self-promote. This is Guerrilla Publishing. You never know how a big break could happen, but you can expect that it will at any moment, then take action every day to be prepared to push your book and your message farther when that moment arrives.

The Scalable System

We are all familiar with Oprah's book club. Being picked for that club is like winning the lottery, guaranteed to drive hundreds of thousands of sales.

In the early book club days, to have your book be considered, or even to be on Oprah as a guest author, meant you had to be ready to deliver at least 300,000 books in one afternoon. This meant only authors with traditional publishers could risk that kind of inventory. Someone like me could never have 300,000 on hand without a guarantee of being on the show. And lead-time for the show would not allow for printing 300,000 at the last minute. The catch-22.

Today, with all honesty I can say, if I am on Oprah, or any other national or international media event that might drive sales of 300,000 books in one appearance, my system will work. People will stream into bookstores and special order, or order them online. I'd hire someone to drop ship all my www.barbarawith.com orders directly to LSI to get fulfilled. At the end of the month, LSI would put all the money in my account ($6.75 (average sales price) x 300,000 = $2,025,000 - $900,000 printing = $1,125,0000).

The odds of this happening get better the longer and more tenacious I become in my commitment to my intention to "take Einstein to the top of the world," my soundbyte for success. But I've never had problems dreaming big. I want to be ready for anything.

If you are ready for anything, anything can happen. If you build it, they can come. Create a little scalable system and you will be ready for it to grow.

The beauty of Guerrilla Publishing is, it doesn't matter if you sell one book or 100,000. Once the system is in place, you never lift a finger to mail a book. The system of printing, distribution, fulfillment, and disbursement takes care of itself. You don't even deposit checks. All you have to do is go out and drive sales and collect money while you sleep. Or not. Your book will be there for the rest of your life, available if you need it or want it for any reason. LSI won't reject it because it's not selling enough.

You decide what level you wish to take your life of a published author. To publish for friends and family won't require a sales and marketing plan. But to really tackle the business of selling books, which means holding events and doing media, you are now ready to launch whatever plan you wish to implement.

In my life, the best opportunities took me by surprise. Getting the number of Oprah's producer was dumb luck. So was being invited out of the blue to appear on a worldwide broadcast to my target audience in 2007. All I did was keep intending to succeed, work hard, pay attention, and be ready.

There is an abundance of resources to promote your book in traditional markets. Bookmasters and Smith Publicity are two that will take your title and include it at the big book expos, list it in catalogues, submit it for reviews and all other typical and standard marketing moves that are expected in the world of publishing. Smith will also work a media campaign, help you develop positioning points and media angles, as well as secure interviews on radio and television, for a price, of course.

The trouble is, you pay someone to take your book to sit on a shelf at an expo in Frankfurt, Germany and that is precisely what it does unless someone can speak up for it and pitch it directly to the thousands of people looking at thousands of new books. You can pay to be listed in the library catalogue, but without a sales call to the librarians who might be perusing it, or a strong presence in your target market, much of this is wasted money.

So how do you approach the sales of your book to fit your own needs and resources? Let me introduce you to the Blue Ocean.

Chapter Eight: Blue Ocean

My literary agent first introduced me to the concept of *Blue Ocean* marketing strategy. The brainchild of W. Chan Kim and Renée Mauborgne of the Blue Ocean Strategy Institute, the idea is simple.

In the "red" ocean of fierce competition of any industry (yours being book publishing) the waters are shark-infested, everyone vying for shelf space, sales, and name recognition. The reason the ocean is red is because of all the blood being spilled as the competitive sharks tear at each other for a piece of the market.

In a "blue" ocean, you create uncontested market space somewhere other than the obvious, where there is no competition. Since there are no sharks, the waters are clear and blue. You have just removed yourself from the market of all your competitors and placed yourself in a new market where no one has what you are offering.

The best example for Blue Ocean I can cite is Cirque du Soleil. They began as a circus, but someone "Blue Ocean-ed" them into an entirely new market where there were no circuses: theater. Broadway had no circus troupes, so Cirque du Soleil created a Broadway show to fit this Blue Ocean. They combined the circus with opera, and removed stars and animal acts. The results speak for themselves. They have since grown their brand to have multiple troupes that perform in theaters around the world.

The idea of removing yourself from the traditional book publishing market and finding a new market where there are no authors or ones in your genre will require some creative thinking. It took me quite a while of brainstorming to come up with my Blue Ocean.

I started by identifying my traditional competition: metaphysical or spiritual authors. In this red ocean are a laundry list of names of authors who have written about my topics: Deepak Chopra, Marianne Williamson, Greg Braden, Sylvia Brown, Jane Roberts, the list goes on. I asked myself, what do I have that these others don't have? I realized it was my extensive experience composing music and performing on stage in rock bands.

That was when I realized my Blue Ocean. It wasn't necessarily moving out of the market, but positioning myself as from a different market. Instead of being an expert in spirituality who also happened to be a musician, I returned to my roots and became a rock and roller who just happened to stumble upon becoming a psychic and eventually the alleged posthumous voice of Albert Einstein.

This slight distinction allowed me to build a compelling and unique personality and brand that would stand out in the metaphysical and traditional publishing market. In rock and roll, you go on tours playing your music; your events (concerts and club gigs) make people want to get up and dance; you dress provocatively and are expected to use colorful language. Rock and roll is all about celebrating, passion, spontaneity, and dancing. Who doesn't want to be a rock star? Woo hoo!

I began to translate this into authorship. How could I use this attitude to sell books and get my message across?

Rebellion

Rock and rollers are known to be rebellious. They bring us back to being teenagers. I took this attitude in everything from cover design to fashion for my promotional shots. *Party of Twelve* was purposefully designed like *Catcher in the Rye*. The title, *Imagining Einstein: Essays on M-Theory, World Peace & the Science of Compassion* is meant to turn heads. Science is a Blue Ocean in the spiritual market; a psychic is a Blue Ocean in the science market.

One of my favorite promotional shots was taken with me in the leopard mini-dress and red high heels holding my laptop like a guitar. My website is wild and crazy, like a glimpse into the inside of my beautiful rock and roll mind. I call my blog, "Out Of My Mind" and use a photo of me looking a bit delirious.

Culture can try and tell me what to put on my back covers, what to wear as an author, what title will sell more books, but since my Blue Ocean is rock and roll, I am basically expected to say screw you.

Celebration

Rock and roll was born in the 1950s, when life during the cold war was enough to make the passionate want to hang themselves listening to Doris Day and Mel Torme. Elvis came along to shake, rattle and roll everyone into a new age of music. It was all about letting down one's hair and dancing dirty for once in our lives. Feeling our passion, letting it all hang out. By the 60s, the Beatles had blown the entire revolution skyward and the rest is history.

My market depicts the attitude of risk and pushing the envelope. I will not adapt to traditional standards, all in celebration of my unique perspective and personality. I'm also willing to take risks, like claiming to talk to Albert Einstein from beyond the grave. Because of this, people remember me and my work.

To find your own Blue Ocean, take some time to think outside the box. Find the rock and roller inside you waiting to rebel, and celebrate. How does that translate into your genre? How can you convey that passion from whatever story you have to tell? Who is your competition? What makes you different than any of them? How can you incorporate your difference into a Blue Ocean?

The Brand of You

In order to speak in public about your book, you have to know your talking points, and develop a public personality. Some great speakers are pure naturals, but many of us also practice and take serious time to rehearse our presentations.

Don't mistakenly think you must be an extrovert to be a good speaker. More than putting on a show, people are also drawn in by authenticity. Actually, authenticity sells much better than hype in the long run.

In marketing, there is a presentation known as an Elevator Speech. That's because if you ever find yourself in the elevator with Oprah, you have about thirty seconds to pitch your idea as concisely and passionately as possible before she gets to her floor.

In order to prepare for the Elevator Speech, begin with a one-page synopsis of what your book is about. Edit that down to a half page, and eventually whittle the message of your book into one or two sentences.

My elevator speech for *Party of Twelve: The Afterlife Interviews* is, "Interviews with twelve famous dead people working together in Afterlife for world peace. Each brings an aspect of 20th century culture, with new insights and revelations from where they are now."

Diaries of a Psychic Sorority is "the true story of three ordinary women, brought together by their 'Angels' to learn a process for world peace, one person at a time, starting with self."

The more concise and articulate you can be, the better able you can name-drop your book and secure media interviews that sell books and begin your name recognition.

Events

One of the easiest events to book is a bookstore book signing, especially area bookstores looking for local authors. Your appearance to speak on your topic or do a reading of your work costs the bookstore nothing, and they only pay for the books you sell.

Go to the websites of the major storefront booksellers like Barnes & Noble and Borders, and check at the bottom for the "Publishers & Authors" link. They provide you with all the forms and information on how to get into their system. You have to be in the system to book an event at a store. But once you are in, you can begin making calls to any store in the country.

If your topic is a self-help or inspirational genre, create an event to demonstrate your process, or prepare a speech to inspire people to change their lives. Perhaps you've written a book about blending AA and meditation. Think of all the AA groups you could attend and offer your book. Or contact the local spiritual bookstore and sell yourself as an expert on using meditation to stop drinking.

At the very least, you can read directly from your book and talk about what inspired you, give insights into how you built the characters, or anecdotes of your writing experience.

Not everyone is as much of a performer as I am. If you have angst about public speaking, I highly recommend Toastmasters. This amazing organization has been around since 1924 and has helped millions of people learn better communication and leadership skills. The fees are about $60 for a year and they have memberships worldwide.

Traditional Venues

There are many avenues to market yourself—press releases, book reviews, catalogues, finding niche distributors, creating a blog, publicity stunts, talk radio, a regular newsletter to an online fan base. Find the things that work for you.

There are several services that provide all the tools to create a mailing list sign-up on your website and then send out newsletters or email advertising to it. I use one called iContact that manages the list (won't allow duplicates, sets up the options to unsubscribe, etc.) and has easy-to-use tools to create the pages. Knowing how to build a webpage comes in handy here, but you can do it using their templates as well. It costs me $27 a month.

I rarely buy advertising unless it's in a program of an event I am appearing at; I do, however, make sure to list in free calendar listings in the cities in which I'm appearing. Talk radio is fun and they are always looking for new and interesting guests to do twelve minutes during drive time. There are lists you can buy of all media outlets, including radio, television, newspapers, magazines, all with contact information and where to send press releases. Writing letters to the editor around your topic can get attention.

Start small. Local morning television or radio talk shows are always in need of new guests. Don't be afraid to call the station and inquire about being on the show. I was once in a meeting with Tene for my non-profit at the local

ABC affiliate station that was sponsoring a WomenVenture event. In passing I happened to mention to the station manager that I was an author of the book *Party of Twelve: The Afterlife Interviews*. Turned out she was a huge Elton John fan, to whom the book is dedicated. Name-dropping my book in that moment got me a spot on the KQ Morning Show in Minneapolis with Tom Bernard, the number one drive-time radio show in the country with a reputation for skewering their guests with sarcasm.

When family, friends and fans heard I was going to be on KQ, a hushed silence would fall, and the looks on their faces became somber and concerned. "Barb," they all said, "He's going to crucify you, you know that, right?"

I spent hours rehearsing my talk. I knew the best defense would be a great offense. I would decide where the conversation would go.

The interview began with me pronouncing how skeptical I am of psychics (Blue Ocean: the skeptical psychic). I grew up in the 60s watching Uri Geller bend spoons. I didn't doubt he could bend them; I was angry that he had this amazing telekinetic power and used it to bend spoons. I made fun of John Edward (the Long Island psychic who became famous for talking to dead people), and within the first two minutes the entire morning crew was on my side. The interview was heard by hundreds of thousands of people and boosted my sales.

Remember the movie, *King of Comedy*. with Jerry Lewis and Robert Deniro? Deniro had an entire late-night talk show set in his mom's basement, and was obsessed with Lewis, who played a Johnny Carson-type. Deniro practiced every night for the day he would get to be on Lewis' show. As nutty as it sounds, this is what you may wish to do (perhaps without the entire Tonight Show set in your basement). Rehearse your talk, develop a character, even if it's just plain you. Be authentic, but don't be afraid to super size a bit. We want them to remember you.

Now that you are a published author, let your vision and your book guide you. Maybe now that you have your book in your hands, you are happy using it in your work and your community. Maybe you suddenly feel a rush of inspiration to get it into the world. Between traditional outlets, the power of the Internet, and utilizing Guerrilla Publishing skills, the possibilities are endless to create a system that works for you.

When I first launched *Einstein* in 2007, I decided to commit to five years to get to the top of whatever heap I was going after. I had no idea how I would do it, but I committed to five years of full bore. I tried not to worry about the bottom line; every book was a calling card. This was about building name recognition.

Shortly before my launch date, someone at my church passed my book on to a man who hosted international events and live monthly podcasts broadcast worldwide. He had a following of about 300,000. After having *Einstein* on his bedside table for months, he finally read it and simply had to have me appear at one of his major events in Taos, New Mexico.

From that one event, which was broadcast live, I received invitations to appear around the world. He and his wife also invited me to travel the world with them. I chose Bucharest and Budapest. From those gigs has come more work than I know what to do with.

How did I do it? Again, a certain amount of dumb luck mixed with hard work, being ready and paying attention. Because a gal from church thought to pass my book along (and what inspired her?), I now speak and conduct workshops internationally.

I have a host in the cities I am appearing in, and in exchange for their help I pay them 30% of registrations for the workshop, free attendance, a set of my books, and a private consultation with me. It's amazingly easy to have events in Europe with people in the city doing the local legwork. I take the registrations online via Paypal, while they find the venue and market in their network.

So far, I have been to Copenhagen, Frankfurt, Oslo several times, Canada, Bucharest, Budapest, Brasov, with invitations standing to Israel, Bulgaria, Australia, New Zealand and Spain on the table. I even got on Norwegian television and sold more books and workshops than ever before.

Four years ago, I could not have told you all that would happen, but I can tell you I fully intended it, every step of the way. Woo hoo.

Epilogue: If You Build It, They *Can* Come

Becoming a published author is a major achievement. I hope when you have your book in your hands and your scalable system in place, you will take some time to revel in your accomplishment. You are now not only a published author, but a Guerrilla Publisher as well.

Be prepared to have people ask you what they have asked me for years, "How do I become a published author?" Now you can inspire them to pick up their power and reach for their dreams as you have yours.

Marianne Williamson once said we are far more afraid of how powerful we are than if we are going to fail. Isn't it strange so many of us are scared to succeed even though we can think of nothing we'd want more?

When you find yourself worrying at any step along the way, stop, take a breath, and re-state your intention. "I fully intend to become a published author. I have no idea how I will accomplish this but I fully intend to learn as I go."

Remember, life is not a dress rehearsal. Passion is your birthright; expressing your creativity is essential for good health and long life. Dream big, set your intention, and who knows where your new book will lead you?

Wherever it is, it's sure to be exciting!

Rock on!

Barbara With is an international peace activist, award-winning author, composer, performer, psychic, workshop facilitator and inspirational speaker living in northern Wisconsin and Corpus Christi, Texas. Her other books include *Imagining Einstein: Essays on M-Theory, World Peace & The Science of Compassion, Party of Twelve: The Afterlife Interviews, Party of Twleve: Post 9/11* and *Diaries of a Psychic Sorority.* She researched and developed Conflict REVOLUTION®, a revolutionary new way for dealing with conflict of the psyche and conducts workshops around the world. She also has two CDs of original music, *Innocent Future* and *Solitaire*.

To schedule a Guerrilla Publishing workshop,
visit www.barbarawith.com or email barbara at
barbarawith11@aol.com